The History of Food

CRAFTED BY SKRIUWER

At **Skriuwer**, we're more than just a team—we're a global community of people who love books. In Frisian, "Skriuwer" means "writer," and that's at the heart of what we do: creating and sharing books with readers worldwide. Wherever you are in the world, **Skriuwer** is here to inspire learning.

Frisian is one of the oldest languages in Europe, closely related to English and Dutch, and is spoken by about **500,000 people** in the province of **Friesland** (Fryslân), located in the northern Netherlands. It's the second official language of the Netherlands, but like many minority languages, Frisian faces the challenge of survival in a modern, globalized world.

We're using the money we earn to promote the Frisian language.

For more information, contact : **kontakt@skriuwer.com** (www.skriuwer.com)

Disclaimer:
The images in this book are creative reinterpretations of historical scenes. While every effort was made to accurately capture the essence of the periods depicted, some illustrations may include artistic embellishments or approximations. They are intended to evoke the atmosphere and spirit of the times rather than serve as precise historical records.

TABLE OF CONTENTS

CHAPTER 6: FOOD IN ANCIENT MESOPOTAMIA AND THE LEVANT

- *Barley-based diets and thick stews*
- *Date palms and irrigation systems*
- *Trade routes and temple feasts*

CHAPTER 7: CULINARY TRADITIONS OF ANCIENT CHINA

- *Millet and rice along major rivers*
- *Domestication of pigs and chickens*
- *Social hierarchy and cooking methods*

CHAPTER 8: INDUS VALLEY AND EARLY INDIAN CUISINE

- *Wheat, barley, and urban storehouses*
- *Use of legumes and spices*
- *Terracotta pots and city planning*

CHAPTER 9: FOOD IN ANCIENT GREECE

- *Mediterranean triad: grains, olives, grapes*
- *Symposiums and social dining*
- *Regional differences among city-states*

CHAPTER 10: THE ROMAN EMPIRE AND ITS FEASTS

- *Wheat, olive oil, and wine staples*
- *Garum (fish sauce) and bold flavors*
- *Banquets showcasing Roman wealth*

CHAPTER 11: FOOD IN MEDIEVAL EUROPE

- *Feudal system and manor farming*
- *Pottage, dark bread, occasional meats*
- *Church influence on feast and fast days*

CHAPTER 12: MEDIEVAL MIDDLE EAST AND THE ISLAMIC GOLDEN AGE

- *Irrigation in arid climates*
- *Rice dishes, spices, and yogurt-based sauces*
- *Trade, scholarship, and culinary blending*

CHAPTER 13: THE MONGOL EMPIRE AND THE SILK ROAD

- *Nomadic meat and dairy diets*
- *Dried meats (borts) and kumis*
- *Facilitating cross-continental trade*

CHAPTER 14: FOOD IN PRE-COLUMBIAN AMERICAS

- *Maize, beans, and squash staple crops*
- *Diverse diets of Maya, Aztec, Inca*
- *Nixtamalization and religious feasts*

CHAPTER 15: AZTECS, INCAS, AND MAYAS

- *Chinampas (Aztecs) and terraces (Incas)*
- *Maize-based dishes and ceremonial meals*
- *Potatoes, quinoa, and freeze-drying*

CHAPTER 16: VIKING AGE AND NORTHERN EUROPE

- *Preserved fish and meats in cold climates*
- *Longhouses and community feasts*
- *Raids, trade, and cultural exchange*

CHAPTER 17: RENAISSANCE FOOD IN EUROPE

- *Refined dining and presentation*
- *Italian city-states and ancient influences*
- *Growth of cookbooks and sugar usage*

CHAPTER 18: THE SPICE ROUTES AND THEIR INFLUENCE

- *Demand for pepper, cinnamon, nutmeg*
- *Venetian trade, Arab merchants, Portuguese expansion*
- *Global cultural exchanges via sea routes*

CHAPTER 19: EARLY COLONIAL ERA FOODS

- *The Columbian Exchange of crops and animals*
- *Sugar plantations, cocoa, and coffee*
- *European, indigenous, and African food blends*

CHAPTER 20: FOOD AT THE DAWN OF THE INDUSTRIAL AGE

- *Continuing influence of colonial goods*
- *Early machines (seed drills, canning)*
- *Urbanization and social class diets*

CHAPTER 1

Introduction to Prehistoric Food

Food has always been a part of life that brings people together. In the earliest times, humans did not have farms or big cooking pots. They lived in caves, simple huts, or moved from place to place. This era is often called the prehistoric period. It is a time before people wrote things down. We only have fossils, bones, tools, and some cave paintings to give us clues. Even with those small clues, we learn that food was very important. Early humans needed to eat to survive, just like animals, but their minds helped them try new ways to find and prepare food.

Early humans were not like modern humans. Some were called Homo habilis or Homo erectus. Later, there were also Neanderthals and Homo sapiens. They all lived at different times, but we often group them and call them early humans. They spread out across Africa, and then they began to move to other parts of the world. Wherever they went, they had to find something to eat. So they watched the animals they hunted and the plants they gathered. By following animals, they could move to new areas when local food got scarce.

In this time, there was no concept of a steady home or farmland. People stayed where they could find food. If animals like mammoths or wild cattle moved, the people followed them. If berries were growing in a certain place, the people would go there too. Once the weather changed or food ran out, they packed up their belongings and moved again. This was the basic pattern of life.

Learning to hunt and gather was not easy. People had to watch how animals behaved. They had to learn which plants were safe to eat. They did not have books or schools to teach them. Instead, older members of the group showed younger ones how to do things. Over time, this knowledge grew, and people got better at surviving.

They started to use tools made of stone. At first, these tools were just sharp rocks. Later, they learned to shape the stones into axes, scrapers, and arrowheads. These tools helped them cut meat, remove animal hides, and crack open nuts. With better tools, they could gather more food in less time. Some people even started to use bones to make needles and fishhooks.

One of the biggest changes in prehistoric food came with the discovery of fire. At first, early humans might have come across fire from natural sources like lightning. They might have been scared of it. But at some point, they figured out that fire was very useful. It could scare away dangerous animals, bring warmth at night, and even cook food. Cooked food tastes better and is easier to chew and digest. People who learned to control fire had a big advantage.

Cooking did more than just improve taste. Some experts think that cooking food allowed early humans to get more nutrients in less time. This might have helped their brains grow larger. Larger brains meant they could plan hunts better, communicate with each other, and protect themselves from dangers. We cannot say for sure how quickly these changes happened, but we know that controlling fire was a huge step.

Prehistoric food was not just about meat. Early humans also ate seeds, nuts, fruits, and roots. Gathering plants was important because sometimes hunts failed. If they could not catch an animal, they still needed something to eat. Wild plants also provided different vitamins and minerals. Children might have helped pick berries or gather eggs from bird nests while older adults might have gone after bigger animals.

Over long periods, these people learned about which plants had special properties. Some might have been used as medicines. Some were poisonous and had to be avoided. There was a lot of trial and error. If a plant made someone sick, they learned not to eat it again. This way of passing down knowledge became a key part of survival.

Food was also used for social reasons. Even if we think of them as "cavemen," they had some basic rules and customs. For example, the best hunters might have shared their meat with the rest of the group. This sharing helped build trust and cooperation. People who worked together had a better chance of surviving. Over time, these social bonds grew stronger, and culture took shape.

Early humans faced many challenges. Ice Ages brought cold climates, forcing them to follow herds of animals who moved to warmer areas. Droughts made certain fruits and nuts disappear for a season. But humans adapted. They changed their patterns. They tried new foods and new ways of cooking. Their ability to adapt was a big reason they survived when many other creatures did not.

We do not have recipes from prehistoric times, but we can guess that much of their diet included roasted or charred meat, raw or lightly cooked greens, and handfuls of berries. They might have also roasted insects or small animals like rabbits and birds. Many groups also gathered shellfish along shorelines. Clams, oysters, and fish were high in protein, and they were easier to catch than large land animals.

As people got better at hunting, they took down bigger prey. Before that, maybe they only scavenged meat from animals that died naturally or were killed by predators. But with sharper tools and group strategies, they could coordinate hunts. They might chase animals off cliffs or into traps. Once an animal was killed, they used almost every part of it. The bones could be used for tools, the hide for clothing or shelter, and the meat for eating.

Some groups lived near coastal areas. They found that fish, shellfish, and seaweed were abundant. Others lived in forested regions where nuts, berries, and small game were plentiful. Each group adapted to what the land offered. This is why the prehistoric diet could differ from region to region.

Life was not easy, but food was the center of their daily efforts. People spent most of their day finding, preparing, and eating food. There was no long-term storage in the earliest times. They did not have cans or refrigerators. If they had extra meat, they might try to dry it in the sun, but this was a skill that probably came later. At first, they ate what they caught right away.

Later on, people learned new ways to preserve their food. Drying meat or fish in the sun is one simple method. Smoking food over a fire is another. These methods let them keep food for days or even weeks. That was important for times when hunting was poor or plants were out of season. Over time, these small improvements added up and allowed humans to grow in number.

Prehistoric people also formed small groups or bands. Each group had its own territory. They did not grow crops yet, so the land had to provide for them naturally. If a territory had lots of animals and plants, it could support more people. If resources were scarce, groups had to stay small or move on.

Communication in these groups was done with gestures, sounds, and later some early forms of language. Sharing knowledge about what to eat and where to find it was vital. If a group discovered a certain valley had many fruit trees in the summer, they would remember and return the next year. This memory passed from older to younger members.

The idea of cooking together also helped create a sense of community. Sitting around a fire could have been a place for telling stories, teaching children, and making plans. Even though we do not have detailed records, we can imagine these simple gatherings as an important part of early social life.

We do not see clear evidence of planned farming in this period. People just did not know how to plant seeds and grow them on purpose yet. Some seeds might have started to sprout near their campsites, but they did not fully understand how to make it happen on a larger scale. That discovery would come much later, and it would change the world forever.

Before we move on, let us note that prehistoric people lived in many different climates. Some lived in cold areas covered in ice. Others lived in warm, lush forests. Their food supplies varied. Yet the main theme is the same: they hunted, gathered, used fire, and shared. This is the big picture of food in the prehistoric era.

CHAPTER 2

Early Gathering Methods and Simple Tools

In the previous chapter, we saw that early humans relied on hunting and gathering. They followed wild game and collected fruit, nuts, and seeds. But how exactly did they gather their food? What tools did they use? This chapter will dive deeper into how simple tools and gathering methods developed. We will look at how people figured out ways to make the best use of their environment without modern technology.

At first, gathering was simply bending down and picking up what looked edible. People might stumble upon a bush full of berries or a tree dropping nuts. But as time went on, they became more skilled at recognizing which plants were worth the effort. They learned to find the best times of year to collect certain seeds or nuts. They found that some plants ripened at different times, so if they planned their movements, they could gather food more often.

For hunting, the earliest humans might have started with just their hands and rocks. Trying to catch a small animal without a real weapon is dangerous, and large animals could be even more dangerous. So they learned to use pointed sticks. Later, they learned to shape stone to make sharp edges. This helped them cut meat off bones and also helped them craft better spears.

Stone tools were very important. Many archaeologists talk about the Stone Age, which is a long period divided into parts like the Paleolithic (Old Stone Age) and Mesolithic (Middle Stone Age). We do not need to get too technical, but it helps to know that in the Paleolithic era, humans began making simple stone flakes or choppers. Over thousands of years, they improved their skills. They discovered better types of stone, such as flint, which could be chipped to form very sharp edges.

One common type of tool was a hand axe. It was shaped like a teardrop and was held in the hand. It could chop wood, break bones, and cut meat. This meant hunters could process more of the animal after a kill. They could cut off pieces to carry back to their camp. The bones themselves might be broken to get marrow, which was full of nutrients.

Early gatherers also learned which parts of plants were edible. Sometimes leaves are good, sometimes roots, and sometimes the fruit or seeds. They experimented with the wild grains that grew in certain areas, though they did not farm these grains yet. They might have roasted them over a fire or ground them between stones to make some kind of rough flour. This flour could then be mixed with water and cooked on a hot rock, forming a primitive bread.

While we do not have written records of these experiments, we find evidence in stone tools that show wear marks. This tells scientists that people were grinding seeds or nuts. We also find plant remains near ancient hearths, suggesting that certain grains were cooked. This was not organized farming, but it was an early step in understanding how plants could be changed or processed for easier eating.

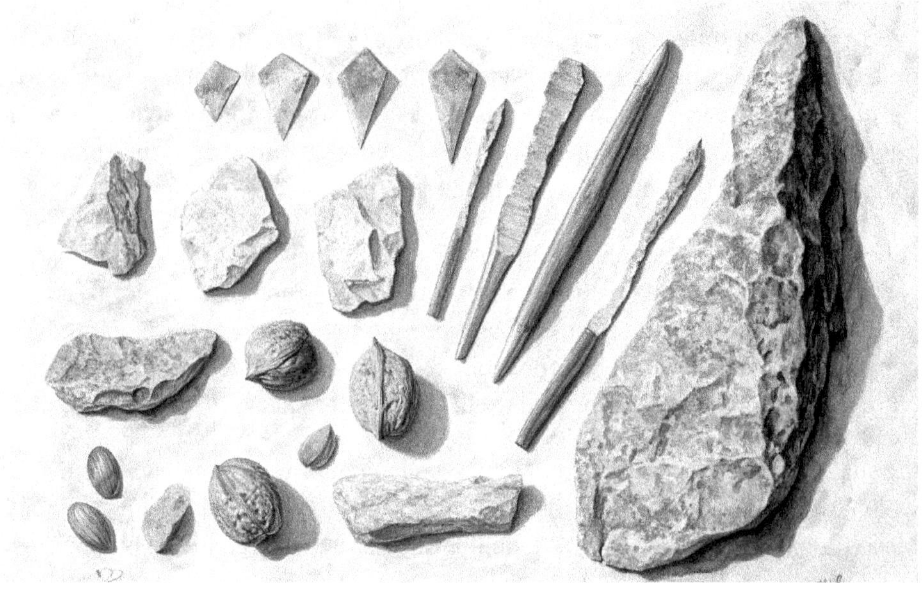

Another method of gathering involved searching along riverbanks and shores. Many coastal and riverside communities found shellfish, small fish, and edible seaweed. They might use sharp sticks to pry open shells or to dig clams out of the sand. As time went on, they made simple nets or weirs (barriers in the water) to trap fish. These nets could have been woven from plant fibers or animal sinews.

Group cooperation was essential. One person alone might struggle to catch a fast-moving deer, but a group of people could succeed by coordinating. They would take advantage of the animal's tendency to run in certain directions or use natural features like cliffs or narrow passes. Once the animal was cornered, a skilled hunter could land a fatal blow with a spear or throw a stone-tipped projectile.

We often think of big game like mammoths or buffalo. While these hunts did happen, they were risky. Early people may have sometimes scavenged from these large animals if they found them dead or wounded. Actual hunts of very large animals took a lot of planning and skill. By contrast, smaller animals like rabbits, deer, or wild boar were more common targets. They also offered enough meat to feed a small band.

Moving on from hunting, we can look at how early humans started to store their food. They had no pottery at first, so they might have used animal skins or woven baskets. Dried gourds could be hollowed out to hold water or seeds. While these items do not usually survive thousands of years in the ground, we have some evidence in cave paintings and rare finds.

Simple preservation methods began to appear. Drying meat in the sun was a popular way to keep it from spoiling right away. Smoking meat over a fire also helped, though that required building some structure to hold the meat. People noticed that smoked or dried food lasted longer. That meant they could have food for a journey or for colder months.

Knowledge about food and tools was passed down mostly by example. Young people learned by watching elders gather nuts or cut meat. Skills like knapping (striking stone to shape it) took practice. Over the generations, the tools improved, and so did their strategies for finding and keeping food.

But life was not stable. Large changes in climate could force groups to move. If an area became too cold or too dry, the plants and animals would change, and people had to adapt. They might move south to find warmer areas or learn to hunt different animals, like reindeer, in colder climates. This is one reason why humans spread across the planet.

Along the way, some groups encountered others. They might share ideas about how to craft better arrowheads or which plants were safe to eat. They might also compete for resources. Food was always a reason for tension if two groups wanted the same territory. But in many cases, sharing knowledge helped both groups survive.

Over time, simple tools advanced. In some places, people started making microliths, which are very small stone blades set into wooden or bone handles. These made spears or arrows more effective. They also could be used as cutting edges for slicing meat or plants. With these improved tools, hunts became more successful. This led to more food, which in turn could support slightly larger groups.

Gathering methods also became more sophisticated. Women, men, and children might each have had certain tasks. For instance, men might focus on larger game hunts, while women might gather tubers, fruits, and seeds, and also look after the children. This division of labor is not a strict rule, as it likely varied among different groups, but it is a common pattern observed by anthropologists studying more recent hunter-gatherer societies.

It is important to remember that early humans did not understand nutrition in the modern sense. They did not know about vitamins or calories. They just knew they felt better when they ate a variety of foods, and they learned which foods gave them energy. They knew some foods were dangerous. Over time, they learned to avoid harmful mushrooms or berries.

Seasonal changes played a big role in what was available. In warmer months, berries and fruits might be everywhere. In colder months, animals might migrate or hide. People had to plan. If they could store a bit of extra food, they had a better chance of surviving the winter or dry season. This planning became a key skill in human survival.

Small improvements in toolmaking led to things like bone needles. With these needles, people could stitch animal hides together to make warmer clothes or better shelters. This had an indirect effect on food gathering because it let them survive in harsh climates. They could go out hunting or gathering in conditions that might have been impossible before.

As groups improved their tools, they sometimes tested new materials. Besides stone and bone, they might use antlers, ivory (from mammoths or elephants), and even shells. Each material had different properties. Bone or antler tips could be very strong and slightly flexible, making them good for spear points.

All of these early methods—gathering, hunting, making tools, preserving food—laid the groundwork for what would eventually become agriculture. But that big leap was still a long way off. For now, most groups preferred to remain nomadic. They went wherever food was most plentiful. If an area became overhunted or if plants were picked clean, they moved on. It was a natural cycle that let the land recover over time.

It is also worth noting that even in areas with abundant resources, people still traveled. They followed animal migrations or moved to find minerals for tools. Gathering different plants at different elevations or latitudes might require seasonal movements. This traveling lifestyle made sense at that time. There was no reason to stay in one place and risk losing all your resources if they became scarce.

At some point, people discovered that seeds dropped near their camps might grow into the plants they liked to eat. But in these earliest stages, it was probably just a happy accident. They did not yet see the big picture. They had no notion of sowing large fields. Instead, they just noticed that some favorite plants showed up again next year. They might protect these growing plants from animals or weeds, but it was not systematic farming.

Still, the main way to get food was to gather wild plants or hunt wild animals. Being able to shape stones into more precise tools gave people the edge they needed to hunt more effectively and expand into various environments. This expansion is one of the reasons we find human remains and artifacts all over the globe.

As the Ice Ages came and went, sea levels changed, and land bridges opened or closed. Humans took advantage of these shifts to move into new territories. Each new territory meant learning about new food sources. Perhaps they encountered different wild grains, fruits, fish, or game. Each group adapted in slightly different ways, leading to a variety of tool styles and gathering techniques.

One of the most critical parts of these gathering methods was cooperation. Gathering large amounts of nuts or grains is easier if multiple people help. This also made it simpler to move heavy items like big chunks of meat or logs for the fire. People would share the load and share the final meal. This sense of sharing was key to survival in tough times.

As we near the end of this chapter, it is important to remember that prehistoric humans lived in a world where nature was both the provider and a threat. Wild animals could attack them if they were not careful. Storms, droughts, and freezing winters could make life very hard. Their success in surviving depended on learning the land's patterns, improving tools, and working together to find food.

These simple methods—like poking at the ground with a sharp stick, throwing a stone-tipped spear, or gathering berries in a basket—might seem small. But they formed the base of everything that came later. Without these first steps, humans would never have moved on to farming, domesticating animals, or creating stable settlements.

In the next chapters, we will see how people eventually moved from this hunting and gathering lifestyle to something new. But it did not happen overnight. Many groups stayed hunters and gatherers for thousands of years, and some still do in remote areas. For most of history, though, it was the main way people got their food. Then, in certain parts of the world, something changed. People began to plant seeds on purpose. They also learned to tame certain animals. This shift marks the beginning of a new era in food history.

So, to wrap up Chapter 2, we can say that early gathering methods and simple tools were a big leap forward in human progress. People learned how to find different kinds of food in many environments. They used stone, bone, and wood to create tools that improved their ability to hunt, gather, and preserve what they found. This period laid the foundation for the next major change in human life: farming.

CHAPTER 3

Farming Begins – The Fertile Crescent

When we look at the story of how people started to farm, the Fertile Crescent is one of the first places we can explore. This region got its name from its shape and from the rich soil found there. It stretches across parts of modern-day Middle East, but we will not focus on the modern countries; we will instead imagine the landscapes thousands of years ago. The Fertile Crescent covered land around the Tigris and Euphrates Rivers, as well as areas near the Jordan River and the eastern Mediterranean coast. This place is often called the birthplace of agriculture.

Before people in this region began farming, they were hunters and gatherers, just like people in many other parts of the world. They traveled with the seasons and found wild game and plants. But something started to change: they noticed that some plants, especially wild grains, grew in abundance near the rivers. When the weather changed, these plants dried, and their seeds fell onto the ground. Sometimes, those seeds sprouted the next year in the same place.

Over countless generations, people learned that if they put seeds in the ground on purpose, they could expect plants to grow there later. At first, this might have happened accidentally. For example, a group might have thrown leftover seeds on the ground near their camp or noticed plants growing around garbage piles. Slowly, they connected the dots: seeds in the ground plus water and good soil equals more of the plants they wanted to eat.

This realization may seem small, but it led to one of the biggest changes in human history. People started to spend part of the year caring for these wild grains. They discovered that by giving the seeds a bit of attention—clearing rocks, removing weeds, and making sure the soil stayed loose—they could improve their harvest. Even though these early efforts were not like modern farming, they represented a huge step away from pure hunting and gathering.

Why Did Farming Take Root in the Fertile Crescent?

The Fertile Crescent was special because of its climate and geography. Rivers like the Tigris and Euphrates brought water and silt that made the soil rich. Even though the area could be dry at certain times, the floodwaters in wetter seasons helped crops to grow. Also, many wild ancestors of today's grains, such as wheat and barley, were native to that region. People did not need to import these plants from far away; they were already there in the wild.

Early farmers also found legumes like peas and lentils, which grew well in the same climates. This combination of grains and legumes gave people a more balanced diet. On top of that, once some animals started to be domesticated (which we will see in the next chapter), people had access to meat and milk as well. But in Chapter 3, we focus mainly on the plant side of agriculture.

From Camps to Early Villages

Once people realized they could grow their own plants, they began to stay longer in one spot. They built more permanent shelters, sometimes out of mud bricks or stones. Small villages formed around these early fields. This shift is known by terms like the "Neolithic Revolution," but we will keep it simple and just say it was the time when farming began.

Staying in one place had consequences for food. On the good side, if the crops did well, there was a reliable source of food each year. On the bad side, if drought or disease hit the crops, the entire community could suffer. People learned to save some seeds from each harvest to plant the following year. This seed-saving practice was important. It meant they looked for the best grains—the ones that were healthier or bigger—and saved them for planting. Over many generations, this led to changes in the plants themselves, making them more suitable for human use.

For instance, wild wheat often shatters easily, scattering its seeds to the ground. This helps the plant reproduce in nature. But for humans, it is easier to harvest wheat that holds onto its seeds until they are collected. So, over time, by planting seeds from the wheat that did not shatter as easily, people ended up with domesticated wheat that was simpler to harvest. Similar patterns happened with barley, peas, and other crops.

The Work of Farming

Farming was not an instant ticket to an easy life. It required hard labor, such as clearing rocks and weeds, digging the soil, planting seeds, and protecting the crops from animals or pests. People needed to water the plants if there was not enough rain. In some places, they dug channels to direct river water into their fields. This early irrigation was another major development. It let them grow crops in areas that might otherwise be too dry.

During harvest time, people used simple stone tools, such as sickles or flint blades, to cut the grain. Then they had to thresh the grain to separate the edible parts from the chaff. Threshing could involve beating the grain or letting animals walk over it. Afterward, they winnowed it by tossing it into the air so the wind would blow away the lighter chaff. All these steps had to happen before they could store the grain in baskets, clay pots, or storage pits.

Storing food was also a new challenge. If they kept grain in a damp place, it could rot or grow mold. If they did not protect it from rodents, mice could eat it. So people learned to build raised platforms or clay structures that kept grain sealed and safe. This was a big change from the days when there was little reason to store large amounts of food, because groups were always on the move. Now, with settled life, storage technology became crucial.

Early Settlements and Community Life

As farming spread in the Fertile Crescent, more groups adopted this way of life. Villages grew. People had to cooperate to manage irrigation systems or to decide when and where to plant. They also found themselves dealing with new conflicts, such as who owned which piece of land or water source. Over time, leadership structures emerged, though this chapter will not dive deep into politics. We just note that the rise of farming led to the growth of more complex social systems.

Houses in these early farming villages were usually small and built close together. Walls might have been made of mud bricks that dried in the sun, while roofs could be layered thatch or woven mats. In some areas, houses were partly underground to keep them cool in hot summers. People decorated their living spaces with simple items made of clay or bone. They also developed basic pottery skills to make cooking pots and storage jars.

These early farmers did not abandon wild foods entirely. Many still hunted gazelle, deer, and small game or fished in rivers. They also gathered wild fruits, nuts, and herbs to add variety to their meals. However, the core of their diet increasingly came from farmed grains and legumes.

A Changing Diet

With farming, the daily meals began to change. Grains like wheat and barley could be ground into flour using stone querns or mortar and pestle. This flour was then mixed with water to make dough. The dough could be baked on flat stones, resulting in the earliest types of bread or flatbreads. This bread might have been coarse and gritty by modern standards, as tiny bits of stone from the grinding process often ended up in the dough. Still, it provided a reliable source of energy and nutrition.

Legumes, such as peas and lentils, became a common protein source, especially before animal domestication became widespread. People could boil them in clay pots over a fire, making simple stews or porridges. Adding wild herbs and any available meat would make the meal more filling. This mix of grains, legumes, and occasional meat laid the groundwork for ancient diets.

The Spread of Farming

From the Fertile Crescent, farming knowledge spread outward in many directions. Over thousands of years, it reached other areas in Asia, Europe, and Africa. People would carry seeds with them, or they would share them with neighboring groups. Sometimes, new settlers moved to fresh lands and brought their farming methods along. In other cases, local hunters and gatherers saw the benefits of growing crops and adopted the practices themselves.

This spread did not happen in a quick or simple way. Different regions had their own climates and native plants, which meant people had to adapt. But the Fertile Crescent remains one of the earliest known centers of agriculture, where domesticated wheat, barley, and legumes first flourished.

Life Was Not Always Easy

Farming life was a big change, but it also brought challenges. If a harvest failed, entire communities could starve. In earlier hunter-gatherer times, if an area's plants or animals disappeared, people might just move elsewhere. But once they built villages, they were more tied to the land. They had to work harder to protect their crops. Also, living close together meant diseases could spread more easily, a problem that was less common among smaller, mobile bands.

Still, despite these hardships, farming offered a more predictable supply of food most years. Over time, people in farming villages began to have surpluses. A surplus means having more food than you immediately need. Surpluses allowed some members of the community to do other tasks besides constantly searching for food. They could specialize in tool-making, pottery, weaving baskets, or other crafts. This specialization would later lead to the development of more complex societies.

Early Rituals and Beliefs

We do not know exactly what people believed in those days, but evidence suggests that agriculture came with new rituals. People might have prayed or performed dances for rain or for healthy crops. Certain symbols, figurines, or carvings might have represented fertility or growth. The cycle of planting and harvesting was closely linked to the seasons, so people observed the changing weather carefully. They noted the positions of the sun and stars, trying to predict when to plant.

In some early settlements, archaeologists have found special rooms or buildings that may have served as temples or communal gathering spots. Inside, there could be paintings or carvings of animals and plants. These discoveries hint that people were connecting food production with spiritual or communal practices.

Looking Beyond the Fields

Although the main theme of this chapter is farming in the Fertile Crescent, we should remember that farming also began independently in other parts of the world. For example, people in China would later farm millet and rice, and people in the Americas developed maize and other crops. We will explore some of these developments in later chapters. For now, we focus on the idea that in one of the earliest farming regions, the Fertile Crescent, humans took a giant leap from gathering wild grains to planting and harvesting them on purpose.

Tools for Farming

Early farmers in this region used tools that might still look familiar in basic form. Sickles, made by setting small stone blades into a wooden or bone handle, helped harvest grain. Hoes and digging sticks helped loosen soil for planting. Simple bone or wooden spades could also be used to move earth around. Stones or pounding tools crushed grain into flour. Even though the materials were simple, the designs were effective for small-scale fields.

People also used large grinding stones or querns. Often, a flat or slightly curved base stone was set on the ground. A top stone, held in the hand, was used to grind the grains. This process took time and effort, which is why bread and porridge in these early days might have been very rough in texture. Over time, people found ways to improve grinding, such as making the stones bigger or using better-fitting surfaces.

CHAPTER 4

Domestication of Animals

As we learned in the previous chapter, early farming communities in places like the Fertile Crescent began to grow and harvest grains, legumes, and other plants. But their relationship with animals also started to change. During the long era of hunting and gathering, animals were mostly viewed as wild game to be hunted or predators to be avoided. Now, with the rise of farming, humans slowly figured out how to domesticate certain animals—turning them into reliable sources of food and useful labor.

Early Closeness with Animals

Even before domestication, humans had formed some basic connections with animals. Hunters observed animal behaviors and knew their movements. Gatherers found animal eggs, skins, or bones to use for clothing or tools. As people began to settle in villages, they noticed that certain animals—especially goats, sheep, and pigs—often gathered around human refuse piles or farmland, attracted by leftover scraps and young plants.

Over time, villagers realized they could corral these animals or pen them in simple enclosures. At first, this might have been done to keep them from harming crops. Later, people discovered the benefits of keeping animals near them. For instance, a goat could provide milk, a sheep could offer wool, and pigs could help eat kitchen scraps. This was far more predictable than hunting for random wild herds, which might not always be around.

Which Animals Were Domesticated First?

Experts think goats and sheep were among the earliest. They were relatively small, easy to handle, and provided multiple benefits (meat, hides, wool, and, in the case of goats, milk). Pigs might have been domesticated around the same time in some regions, although pigs may not have been as easily herded over long distances. Cattle came a bit later, as they are larger and can be harder to manage. However, once domesticated, cattle became hugely important for plowing fields and providing a steady supply of milk and meat.

It is important to remember that domestication is a process. It did not happen in a single day or year. People first had to capture wild animals, keep them alive in captivity, and breed them. Over many generations, the tamer animals that were less fearful of humans (and possibly more docile) were the ones that survived and reproduced. Eventually, these animals changed physically from their wild ancestors. For example, domesticated sheep grew thicker wool, and domesticated goats often became smaller and tamer than the wild versions.

The Benefits of Domestication

1. **Meat on Demand**: Rather than chase animals across the landscape, people could have a flock of sheep or goats near their settlement. When they needed meat, they could slaughter an animal.

2. **Milk and Dairy Products**: Goats, sheep, and cattle all produce milk. While it may have taken time for people to figure out they could drink milk from these animals, once they did, it added an important source of nutrients to their diet. Over time, people learned to make simple cheeses or yogurts, though these earliest dairy products may have looked very different from what we have today.

3. **Fiber and Hides**: Sheep provided wool that could be spun into thread and turned into textiles. Animal hides could be turned into leather for clothing, shoes, and containers.

4. **Labor**: Larger animals like cattle could pull simple plows (once plows were invented) or carry heavy loads. This greatly increased the amount of land people could farm and reduced the manual labor required for tasks such as hauling water or goods.

5. **Fertilizer**: Animal dung could be used to enrich the soil, helping crops grow better. Over time, farmers saw that fields manured by their animals produced healthier plants.

These benefits meant that domestic animals quickly became a key part of early agricultural life. In fact, the synergy between domesticated plants and animals spurred the growth of villages. Farmers who had animals also had a more varied diet and stronger farmland through natural fertilization.

Changes in Lifestyle and Diet

With animals close by, people had new sources of protein and fat. Meat from a penned animal was sometimes more tender than wild game, as domesticated animals were not running around as much. Milk, butter, and early cheese products provided different flavors and nutrients that were not as common in a strict hunter-gatherer diet.

However, raising animals also brought new challenges. Flocks needed feeding and care. Shepherds had to protect them from wild predators like wolves or lions that roamed the countryside. Diseases could spread through a crowded pen, leading to the death of multiple animals. Managing herds required planning and cooperation among villagers.

Selective Breeding

Just like with plants, humans practiced a form of selective breeding with animals. They kept the animals that were calmer, easier to manage, or that produced more milk or better wool. Over many generations, these traits became more common in the flock or herd. This is why domesticated animals ended up looking and acting differently than their wild ancestors.

For instance, wild sheep might have had coarse hair and some wool, but domesticated sheep were bred to have thick woolly coats. In the case of goats, people likely selected animals that produced more milk or had a friendlier temperament. Over time, certain breeds emerged, each suited to local conditions and needs.

Beyond the Fertile Crescent

While the Fertile Crescent was a major center for early animal domestication, similar processes took place in other parts of the world. For example, in parts of Asia, people domesticated water buffalo and yaks. In Africa, cattle became central to many cultures. In the Americas, people eventually domesticated turkeys and llamas. We will explore some of these regional differences in later chapters. For now, we focus on how domesticated animals grew hand in hand with farming communities in the Near East.

Animal Products and Cooking

In these early villages, cooking changed along with the introduction of farm animals. New dishes involved the use of milk, cheese-like curds, or even early butter, which could be churned by shaking milk in a container made of animal skin. People also started to experiment with bone broth—boiling bones for extended periods to extract nutrients and flavor.

Bones left over from domesticated animals were often used for tools, such as needles, awls, or fishhooks. Horns from goats or sheep could become drinking vessels or simple containers. The entire animal became a resource, which helped people make use of every part. Even blood might have been used in cooking, though we have less archaeological evidence for that.

Impact on Agriculture

It might seem odd to say that animals had an impact on agriculture, but they absolutely did. As people kept animals near the fields, the animals enriched the soil with their manure. Also, when the time came to plow large plots of land, cattle or oxen could help pull early plows. Though the earliest farmers used digging sticks and simple hand tools, eventually they found ways to hitch animals to plows. This allowed them to work bigger fields and grow more crops.

The bigger harvests that followed led to larger populations in the villages. More people, in turn, meant more hands to help with farming and animal care. Over time, this growth fueled the rise of towns and even early cities. While we will not jump too far ahead, it is clear that domestic animals were a major driving force in the development of complex societies.

Challenges of Keeping Animals

While domestic animals were valuable, they also brought certain problems. Keeping many animals in close quarters could attract pests, like fleas or ticks. Where there were animals, predators followed, so villagers had to guard their flocks day and night. Disease could spread from animals to humans or vice versa. This is a trend that continued in later history, but we will not go too deep into modern diseases here.

Another issue was feeding the animals. In dry times or cold seasons, fresh grass or wild forage might be scarce. Farmers had to plan by storing hay or straw to feed their livestock. If the animals starved, the farmers lost a vital source of food and labor. This required forward-thinking strategies, such as growing extra grain or forage crops specifically for the animals.

Early Uses of Animal Power

One of the biggest benefits of domestication, besides food, was harnessing animal power. Although the earliest stage of domestication was mostly about meat, milk, and fiber, people soon saw that a strong ox or a pair of cattle could be used to pull heavy loads. They likely began by using animals to help in building projects—dragging logs or large stones. Later, they connected a simple wooden plow to the animal, which helped break up soil faster than a person could with a hand tool.

This shift allowed people to cultivate more land, which meant bigger harvests. Over many generations, this led to surplus crops, which in turn supported more complex societies. We will see, in later chapters about places like Mesopotamia and Egypt, how important animal power was for building irrigation canals and other large projects.

Animal Husbandry Skills

Taking care of animals is called animal husbandry. Early farming communities had to learn these skills through trial and error. They discovered how to control breeding, how to recognize sick animals, and how to wean young animals from their mothers so the mothers could keep producing milk for human use. They also needed to understand grazing patterns—when to move animals to a new pasture and how not to overgraze the land, which would ruin it for future use.

Social roles emerged around animal care. Some individuals became experts in caring for sheep and goats; others might have been skilled at handling cattle. This specialization continued to grow as villages expanded. Over time, knowledge about animals was passed down through families or taught to new members of the community.

Cultural and Spiritual Roles of Animals

Animals were not just food; they often played a role in spiritual life. Some early religious or ceremonial practices involved animals as offerings to gods or spirits. We find bones buried in special pits or under floors in ancient sites, suggesting ritual importance. People might have believed that animal spirits affected their success in farming or hunting.

Certain animals became symbols of fertility or strength. For example, a bull might represent power because of its size and force. A mother goat or sheep with offspring might symbolize fertility and plenty. This ties back to how food and spirituality were linked in early communities. Life depended on successful harvests and healthy animals, so it is not surprising that beliefs and rituals formed around these vital resources.

The Gradual Shift Away from Exclusive Hunting

Hunting did not stop once animals were domesticated. Many people still hunted wild animals to add variety to their diet or to acquire hides and bones from creatures not yet tamed. Wild boar, deer, or certain birds might still be hunted in the forests or marshlands. Yet, as domestic herds grew, reliance on hunting decreased. This freed up time and energy for other tasks, like improving farming techniques, building houses, or making better tools.

Over time, the balance between hunting and herding changed. Some people specialized in herding and rarely hunted at all. Others, especially on the edges of agricultural lands, might have continued to hunt more frequently. These varied lifestyles coexisted for a long period. In some parts of the world, they still do. But in the core regions of early agriculture, domesticated animals became a constant part of village life.

Breeding for Specific Purposes

As more animals were domesticated, people realized they could selectively breed them for specific purposes. For instance, a certain line of sheep might produce better wool. Another might be larger and produce more meat. With goats, some might produce more milk, while others were more robust in harsh climates. Over many generations, this led to early "breeds" of livestock that were suited to different roles or different environments.

Cattle, once domesticated, became incredibly important. A single bull or ox could help plow land faster than several people working by hand. This allowed farmers to expand their fields. The extra grain they produced could feed even more animals, and the cycle continued. This set in motion a pattern of growth that formed the basis of larger settlements and, eventually, more complex societies.

Animal Domestication and Village Layout

Over time, villages adapted their layouts to include pens, barns, or enclosed areas for animals. Living near animals was both convenient and sometimes smelly or unhygienic, so some communities created separate areas for livestock. In archaeological sites, we see evidence of corrals or barns. These might have been made of simple wooden fences or mud-brick walls. Keeping animals safe from predators and preventing them from wandering off was a constant concern.

In many early farming settlements, people also stored fodder for the animals—stalks of harvested plants, dried grasses, or collected hay. This fodder was essential during dry seasons or winters when fresh pasture was unavailable. Storing animal feed required extra buildings or covered areas, adding complexity to the village.

Social Effects of Domestication

As with plants, domesticating animals affected how people related to one another. Owning a large herd could bring wealth or influence. Those who had many animals might trade them or their products—milk, hides, or wool—with others. Trade networks sprang up between villages, allowing them to exchange goods that each specialized in. Over time, these exchanges would grow into larger trade routes, especially once people began to travel more widely with pack animals.

These changes also affected social structures. Some families or groups might become more powerful if they controlled large herds. Inequalities could appear, leading to different classes of people. Again, we will not jump too far into societal development, but it is important to see how the ability to domesticate and breed animals helped shape early human communities beyond just food.

The Daily Use of Animals

On a day-to-day level, a typical early farming family might begin the day by letting their goats out to graze near the village. Someone would watch the flock, guiding them to grassy areas and keeping an eye out for predators. Another family member might gather eggs from domesticated fowl or feed pigs with scraps. Children could have chores such as fetching water for the animals or collecting dung for fertilizer.

Later in the day, villagers might milk the goats or sheep if they had learned how to do so regularly. This milk could be consumed fresh or set aside to turn into a simple cheese or yogurt. If an animal was nearing the end of its useful life, it might be slaughtered for meat and its hide. In this way, animals provided food, clothing materials, and even social status.

Keeping Track of Animals

As herds grew, people needed ways to count them or mark ownership. This might have led to early forms of record-keeping. Some archaeologists suggest that small clay tokens or markings on pottery could be related to counting animals or grain. While we cannot be sure of every detail, it is clear that as animal husbandry became more complex, people needed systems to manage them.

Future Impacts

By the end of this period, the stage was set for major civilizations to rise. Domesticated animals—along with cultivated plants—gave humans a more stable and varied food supply. This stability allowed populations to grow and communities to organize themselves in new ways. Eventually, it would lead to the development of towns, trade networks, and a host of innovations in technology and society.

But let us not rush ahead. In the chapters to come, we will look at how different ancient cultures—like those in Egypt, Mesopotamia, and elsewhere—used both plants and animals in unique ways. We will see how these early steps of farming and herding blossomed into grand agricultural systems, full of new techniques and recipes.

Summary of Chapter 4

In this chapter, we explored how animals moved from being wild game to important parts of daily life in early farming communities. Goats and sheep were among the first to be domesticated, followed by pigs, cattle, and others. Domesticated animals offered a steady supply of meat, milk, wool, and hides. They also became work partners, pulling plows and hauling goods.

This shift to animal husbandry was not always easy. Villagers had to keep animals safe from predators and disease. They needed to store fodder and manage breeding. However, the benefits were huge. Animals gave farmers more stable access to high-protein foods, allowed them to grow more crops thanks to plowing and fertilizing, and provided goods they could trade with neighbors.

By learning to care for animals, humans took another major step forward in controlling their food supply. Hunting still continued, but domestic herds made life more predictable and allowed some members of the community to focus on other tasks. This period laid more groundwork for the future cultures we will study in upcoming chapters.

With the dawn of both farming and animal domestication, the stage was set for the rise of larger, more structured societies. People in different regions began to adapt these ideas, developing their own crops and livestock in accordance with local conditions. In the next chapters, we will see how food developed in some of the most well-known ancient civilizations, starting with places like Ancient Egypt and Mesopotamia, where the rivers shaped daily life and the ways people grew and prepared their food.

CHAPTER 5

Ancient Egypt – Bread, Beer, and the Nile

In the history of food, Ancient Egypt stands out for many reasons. One of the biggest is the Nile River. Every year, the Nile flooded its banks, leaving behind a layer of rich, dark soil. This soil made it easier to grow grains and other crops. Thanks to the Nile's flooding, the people of Ancient Egypt developed one of the most stable food supplies of the ancient world. They also became famous for two main staples: **bread** and **beer**. These were not just snacks or occasional treats; they were at the heart of daily meals for many Egyptians.

Life Along the Nile

Ancient Egypt ran along the banks of the Nile, stretching from the fertile delta in the north to the more arid regions in the south. Although there was desert on both sides, the strip of land close to the river was extremely fertile. Each year, the river overflowed between roughly June and September (the timing could vary). When the waters went down, they left behind silt packed with nutrients.

Egyptians learned to work with this cycle. They planted seeds in the moist ground after the flood, and as the months passed, crops flourished. Wheat and barley were especially important. Harvest time came before the next flood, and farmers stored what they gathered in granaries. Thanks to this pattern, Egyptians had a steady flow of grains for making bread and beer.

The Nile did more than just water the crops. It served as a highway for boats carrying goods. Fishermen caught fish in its waters, adding protein to the Egyptian diet. Reed plants (like papyrus) grew along the banks, which helped in making baskets, mats, and even writing material. Life revolved around the river in countless ways.

Egypt's Social Structure and Food

Many Egyptians were farmers who lived in small villages along the Nile. They worked fields belonging to temples, the royal house, or local landowners. When harvests were good, everyone benefited. But if the floods were too high or too low, it caused trouble. A poor flood could mean less fertile soil, fewer crops, and possible famine.

Food was not divided equally among all people. Wealthy families, priests, and pharaohs had access to better cuts of meat, fruit, and more variety in general. Still, most Egyptians had some version of bread and beer each day, plus vegetables like onions, garlic, and lettuce. They also ate beans, peas, and lentils. Those with more resources could enjoy dates, grapes, figs, and meat from cattle, sheep, goats, and poultry.

Bread in Ancient Egypt

Bread was a cornerstone of the Egyptian diet. When archaeologists study ancient Egyptian tombs, they often find bread loaves or bread molds. This shows how central bread was to daily life and spiritual customs. Egyptian bread could vary in shape and ingredients. Some loaves were round and flat, while others were more dome-shaped. They often used barley or emmer wheat (an ancient kind of wheat), which they ground into flour.

Grinding the Grain: Women usually ground the grain by hand, using a large flat stone on the ground and a smaller handheld stone on top. This method was slow and required a lot of effort. Tiny bits of stone often got mixed into the flour, so Egyptian bread sometimes contained gritty particles that could wear down people's teeth.

Making the Dough: After grinding the grain into flour, they mixed it with water and sometimes yeast or sour dough starter. They might also add salt, herbs, or even honey for flavor if those were available. Once formed, the dough was left to rise, though the rising process might not be as controlled as modern baking.

Baking: Egyptians used clay ovens or open fires to bake bread. In some cases, they placed the dough in tall, conical bread molds, which they heated to bake a loaf inside. Other times, they used flat baking surfaces or cooked the dough in ashes. Because of variations in technique, each household might have had its own unique flavor and style.

Beer: Egypt's Beloved Drink

If bread was the solid base of the Egyptian diet, beer was the liquid cornerstone. In Ancient Egypt, beer was not just for getting drunk. It was a nutritious drink that people of all classes consumed daily. Many times, workers at construction sites (like the ones building pyramids or temples) were paid partly in bread and beer. This shows how beer was essential to the common person's diet.

How They Made Beer: Egyptians commonly brewed beer from barley. First, they baked a type of bread made of half-baked barley dough. Then, they crumbled this bread into jars of water, letting it ferment. Natural yeasts (and possibly leftover yeast from previous batches) helped turn the mix into beer. The result might have been thick and cloudy by modern standards. Drinkers sometimes used straws to avoid large lumps of grain.

Nutrition in Beer: Beer contained calories, some vitamins, and other nutrients, making it more like a liquid food than a simple drink. In a hot climate, drinking beer was often safer than drinking untreated river water. The fermentation process killed some harmful microbes, although it was far from a sterile process.

Social and Spiritual Role: Beer, like bread, had a place in religious ceremonies and offerings to the gods. It was also part of daily meals. Even children drank weaker forms of beer. It was simply viewed as a normal part of life, much like bread was.

Vegetables, Fruits, and Herbs

Besides bread and beer, Egyptians ate a variety of vegetables. Onions and garlic were popular, both for flavor and health beliefs. Lettuce, cucumbers, and leeks appeared in many meals. Wealthier people might have fresh salads or mixed vegetable dishes. Poorer folks still used onions and garlic to spice up simpler meals.

Fruits like dates, figs, grapes, and pomegranates were common for those who could afford them or lived where they grew easily. Dates were especially important—dried dates could last a long time and serve as a sweet treat or a sugar substitute. Farmers along the Nile also grew melons and other fruits to take advantage of the fertile soil.

Herbs and seasonings might include coriander, cumin, and salt. Honey served as a sweetener, especially for wealthier individuals. Ordinary families might not have honey regularly, but they could still gather wild honey if they knew how to handle bees. Later, beekeeping became more organized, but even basic ways of collecting honey have ancient roots.

Meat, Fish, and Poultry

The Egyptians did raise cattle, sheep, goats, and poultry such as ducks, geese, and chickens (introduced in later periods). However, **most** Egyptians did not eat large amounts of meat daily. Meat was costly, so it was more common on special occasions or for wealthier families. Still, fish from the Nile provided a good protein source, especially for those near the river.

Drying and Preserving: With a hot, dry climate, Egyptians could dry fish and meats in the sun to preserve them. They might salt the fish or rub it with spices to keep it from spoiling. This allowed them to store food for times when fresh catch was not available.

Feasts and Festivals: On special feast days or religious festivals, people ate more meat than usual. They might slaughter a goat or sheep, sharing the meat among friends and neighbors. Priests often participated in these feasts, offering parts of the animal to the gods in temple rituals.

Religion and Food

Egyptian religion was deeply linked to nature. Gods and goddesses governed the Nile, fertility, the harvest, and other aspects of daily life. Offerings of bread, beer, fruits, and meats were given to gods in temples. People believed these gifts pleased the gods and ensured continued favor—like a good Nile flood or protection from disease.

Pharaohs, considered gods on Earth, made large donations of food to temples and sometimes distributed rations to the people. Royal tombs and wealthy burials included food offerings, so the dead could eat in the afterlife. This is why archaeologists often find bread loaves, jars of beer, dried meats, and baskets of fruits in tombs.

Cooking Techniques

Egyptians used simple clay ovens, open-fire cooking, and pottery vessels for boiling or stewing. They might fry or roast fish and small cuts of meat. For thick stews, they added vegetables, legumes (like beans and lentils), and sometimes leftover bits of bread. The dryness of the climate meant they had to be mindful of water. Irrigation was mostly for farming, so water for cooking and drinking was precious.

Kitchen Spaces: Many homes had small indoor or outdoor cooking areas. Pottery containers held grains, flours, and spices. Stones served as grinding tools. Wealthier households might have more advanced setups, with multiple jars, baskets, and clay ovens shaped specifically to hold bread. But the basics—fire, pottery, stone grinders—were present in most Egyptian homes.

Feast for All or Food for Some?

Though it might seem like Egyptians enjoyed plenty, not everyone experienced the same abundance. The country was known for surpluses, and it often exported grain to neighboring lands. But these surpluses were managed by officials and stored in state or temple granaries. Ordinary farmers had to meet quotas, often working large estates owned by the temples or the pharaoh. Any leftover might go to the farmer's own household. If floods failed, harvests were small, and famine loomed, hitting common folk hardest.

However, in good years, many people got enough bread, beer, and vegetables to stay healthy. This relative stability is one reason Ancient Egypt endured for so many centuries. Reliable food production and strong organization helped it grow into one of the world's great civilizations.

Legacy of Ancient Egyptian Food

Even though we see Ancient Egypt through the lens of pyramids and pharaohs, food was what fueled the daily life of this civilization. Bread, beer, and the bounty of the Nile created a consistent diet that shaped their culture. Their irrigation methods and storage systems influenced future societies, and their approach to bread and brewing spread across regions.

In summary, Ancient Egypt shows how a river's cycle can shape a civilization's entire food system. With fertile land, a steady grain supply, and a strong focus on bread and beer, Egyptians enjoyed relative stability in their diets. They developed techniques for baking, brewing, irrigating, and storing that were quite advanced for their time.

CHAPTER 6

Food in Ancient Mesopotamia and the Levant

We have learned about the Fertile Crescent and how people first started farming and domesticating animals there. Now it is time to explore two major areas within that region: **Mesopotamia** and the **Levant**. Both areas were home to some of the earliest cities and cultures, each with its own way of growing and preparing food. Mesopotamia lay between the Tigris and Euphrates Rivers, while the Levant included lands along the eastern coast of the Mediterranean Sea. These places were neighbors to Ancient Egypt but developed distinct food habits shaped by their local climate, geography, and trade connections.

Mesopotamia: Land Between Two Rivers

The name "Mesopotamia" literally means "land between rivers." The Tigris and the Euphrates flow from the mountains of what is now eastern Turkey down to the Persian Gulf region. Like the Nile, these rivers flooded, but not as predictably. Farmers in Mesopotamia built canals and irrigation channels to manage water, turning parts of a dry region into fertile farmland.

Civilizations such as Sumer, Akkad, Babylon, and Assyria grew in Mesopotamia. They built cities with temples called ziggurats. They also developed cuneiform writing, which gives us some of the earliest written records about daily life, including references to food.

Crops and Farming Methods

Mesopotamian farmers relied heavily on **barley**, as it could handle the region's heat and sometimes salty soil better than other grains. Wheat was grown as well, but barley remained a staple for making bread and beer. Other important crops included onions, garlic, peas, lentils, cucumbers, and an assortment of herbs.

Farmers also learned to grow **date palms**. Dates provided a sweet fruit that could be eaten fresh or dried, adding sugar to the diet. Date palm groves often lined canals or gardens near the rivers. The leaves of the palms could be woven into baskets or mats, and the trunk wood had building uses as well. This made the date palm a multipurpose plant in Mesopotamia.

Irrigation and Canal Systems

To make the most of the Tigris and Euphrates waters, Mesopotamians dug an extensive network of canals and channels. This water control required cooperation among villagers and later among city-states. Officials managed how water was distributed, sometimes leading to conflicts if one city blocked or diverted water away from another.

Irrigation allowed farmers to plant crops in areas that otherwise would be desert. However, poorly managed irrigation could lead to a buildup of salts in the soil, harming productivity. Over centuries, some fields became too salty to support certain crops, a challenge that Mesopotamians struggled to solve.

Diet in Mesopotamia

Just like in Egypt, bread and beer were central parts of the diet. Barley bread, however, might have been more common in Mesopotamia than wheat bread. Mesopotamians also made a type of beer that was thick and sometimes required a straw. Cuneiform texts mention shipments of barley for brewing, showing how important beer was for daily life and for paying workers.

Mesopotamians also ate vegetables like onions, garlic, turnips, and cucumbers. They enjoyed fruits such as dates, figs, apples (in some regions), and grapes (where they could grow). Meat came from goats, sheep, cattle, and birds, though it was likely a luxury for common people. Fish from the rivers was also a key protein source.

Cooking: Clay ovens, open fires, and clay pots were standard. One famous Mesopotamian text, often called a "cookbook" by historians, contains recipes for different stews. These recipes used ingredients like onions, garlic, leeks, and meats. Spices might include coriander, cumin, or mustard seeds, depending on local availability. They even used dairy products—like milk or yogurt—to make certain dishes thicker.

Social Customs Around Food

In larger Mesopotamian cities, wealthy households could afford a variety of foods and seasonings. Palaces and temples hosted grand feasts, with an array of meats, breads, fruits, and sweet date-based treats. Temples also received food offerings for the gods. Common citizens, on the other hand, ate simpler meals: barley bread, onions or other vegetables, and maybe some fish or goat's milk.

Workers, such as those building temples or city walls, might be paid in barley rations. This barley was then turned into bread or beer. Large storage facilities kept grains to feed the city's population or for trade with neighboring regions.

Food in the Levant

The Levant refers to the lands along the eastern Mediterranean coast, including areas that today would encompass parts of Syria, Lebanon, Israel, Palestine, and Jordan. In ancient times, cities like Ugarit, Byblos, and Jericho thrived there. The climate in the Levant varies, with coastal regions enjoying moderate rainfall and inland areas being drier.

Farming and Gathering: People in the Levant grew wheat, barley, grapes, olives, and figs. They also raised sheep and goats, just like in Mesopotamia. The coastline provided fish and other seafood. Inland areas might rely more on herding animals, while coastal folks took advantage of sea trade and fishing.

Olive Oil and Grapes: Olives were very important in the Levant. They pressed olives to produce oil, which was used for cooking, lamp fuel, and in religious offerings. Grapes were turned into wine, a beverage that became a prized trade item. Over time, wine-making techniques spread across the Mediterranean region.

Trade and Cultural Exchanges

The Levant was a crossroads for trade between Egypt, Mesopotamia, and other nearby regions. Merchants traveled by sea or along caravan routes, bringing goods like spices, incense, textiles, and metals. This trade also exchanged food ideas. New fruits, seeds, or cooking methods might move from one land to another. People in the Levant had access to both Egyptian grains and Mesopotamian barley, as well as their own local produce.

This exchange of goods and ideas enriched Levantine cuisine. Over time, local dishes combined the tastes of many cultures, featuring grains, legumes, olive oil, fish, meat, and a variety of fruits. Salt from the Dead Sea region was another valuable commodity, traded far and wide to preserve food.

Meat, Fish, and Dairy in the Levant

Like elsewhere in the ancient Near East, many ordinary people in the Levant did not eat large amounts of meat regularly. Sheep and goats were more common than cattle, which required more land. Fish was an option in coastal towns or near rivers and lakes. People also raised poultry—ducks, chickens (introduced in later times), and geese—for eggs and meat.

Dairy products from goats or sheep included milk, yogurt, and simple cheeses. Much like Mesopotamia, families used clay pots to cook stews or soups. They might have baked flatbreads on hot stones or in basic ovens, enjoying them with olive oil, herbs, and dips made from legumes like chickpeas.

Religion and Food in Mesopotamia and the Levant

In both Mesopotamia and the Levant, religious practices involved offerings of food to gods and ancestors. Temples stored large amounts of grain, oil, and wine for ritual use. Animal sacrifices might provide meat for priests and participants in religious ceremonies. Feasting was part of many celebrations or festivals, where communities gathered to share food in honor of a deity or a special event.

Spiritual beliefs often tied a god or goddess to fertility of the land. For example, in Mesopotamia, the god Enlil was sometimes associated with wind and agriculture, while the goddess Inanna (or Ishtar) might be linked to fertility and love. In the Levant, various deities governed rain, harvest, and livestock health. People believed that feeding the gods with offerings ensured good harvests and protected the herds.

Writing, Records, and Recipes

Mesopotamians invented a system of writing called cuneiform. They pressed wedge-shaped marks into clay tablets. Some of these tablets have references to ration lists, showing how much barley or oil was given to workers. Others contain what we might call the earliest recipes—instructions for making stews or breads in temple kitchens or palace feasts.

For example, a tablet might say: "Take meat, water, fat, and salt. Add leeks, onions, and garlic. Boil until cooked." These are not detailed like modern recipes, but they give us a glimpse of the ingredients and methods used in ancient Mesopotamian cooking. In the Levant, writing systems developed as well (like the alphabetic scripts), though fewer direct references to recipes have survived. Still, trade documents and inscriptions about offerings tell us about the types of food people valued.

Cooking Tools and Techniques

Across Mesopotamia and the Levant, basic cooking tools included:

- **Clay or metal pots**: for boiling or stewing.
- **Clay ovens**: sometimes dome-shaped or rectangular, used for baking bread.
- **Mortars and pestles**: for grinding spices or grains.
- **Stone grinders**: similar to Egyptian methods, used for flour.
- **Knives and ladles**: likely made from metals like bronze or later iron, though simpler tools could be made from sharpened stones or bones.

Cooking methods involved stewing, boiling, roasting, and sometimes frying in oil. Baking bread was common, with flatbreads being a staple. People seasoned their dishes with herbs, salt, and occasionally sweeteners like date syrup or honey. Over time, as trade expanded, spices from distant lands might have found their way into local markets, enriching the flavor palate.

Beer, Wine, and Other Drinks

Beer was standard in Mesopotamia, often made from barley. In the Levant, **wine** took on a bigger role, especially in the coastal regions suited for vineyards. However, both beer and wine appeared in both regions to some degree, due to trade and cultural exchange.

Water also came from wells, rivers, or collected rainfall. In cities, people might store water in large clay containers. Milk, especially goat or sheep's milk, could be drunk fresh or soured to extend its shelf life. In a hot climate, preserving liquids was important, so fermentation and careful storage were key.

Social Classes and Food Access

As with many ancient societies, the wealthier classes in Mesopotamia and the Levant had access to more variety and quantity of food. Common people worked the fields or herded animals. Their meals were filling but simpler—barley bread, legumes, onions, and some beer or water. Meanwhile, nobles, priests, or merchants might dine on special dishes, more meats, sweet desserts made with honey or date syrup, and imported delicacies.

Temples and palaces often had large kitchens or breweries. These places employed cooks, bakers, and brewers who produced food for ceremonies or for feeding officials and workers. Large storage rooms held grains, oil, wine, or beer that could support a city during tough times or be used in trade.

Regional Dishes and Tastes

While we cannot list exact recipes, we can guess that a typical stew might include barley or wheat, onions, garlic, lentils, and bits of whatever meat was available. Seasonings could include salt, herbs like cumin or coriander, and maybe a splash of sour dairy or wine. Flatbreads dipped in oil or stew formed a hearty, simple meal.

Date-based sweets might be offered at special feasts, combining crushed dates with nuts and honey. This creates a thick, sugary mixture that can be pressed into shapes—an early version of candy or dessert bars. Figs could be dried and stored, often eaten as a quick energy snack or dessert.

Conflicts, Empires, and Food Supplies

Over centuries, city-states in Mesopotamia often fought each other for control of fertile land and water. Empires like Babylon or Assyria expanded, taking over farmland and resources. Yet no matter who ruled, the basic staples—barley, wheat, dates, legumes, goats, sheep, and fish—remained the backbone of the local diet.

In the Levant, shifting powers like the Canaanites, Phoenicians, Israelites, and Arameans influenced the region's cultural blend. Phoenicians, for instance, were famous seafarers, spreading Levantine goods like olive oil, wine, and salted fish around the Mediterranean. Through these travels, Levantine food traditions reached distant shores, blending with local cuisines elsewhere.

CHAPTER 7

Culinary Traditions of Ancient China

Ancient China was home to one of the longest-lasting and most influential civilizations in history. Located in East Asia, it encompassed many types of terrain, from fertile plains and river valleys to mountains and deserts. Food in ancient China developed in fascinating ways, shaped by the vast differences between the north and the south, the abundance of certain crops, and the careful cultivation of land along major rivers. Over time, this region witnessed the growth of rice farming, the use of various grains, and the early domestication of animals like pigs and chickens. In this chapter, we explore the foundation of Chinese culinary traditions, focusing on the ancient period before the modern age.

The Land and Its Rivers

Two major rivers helped shape ancient Chinese agriculture: the **Yellow River** (Huang He) in the north and the **Yangtze River** (Chang Jiang) in the south. Both rivers flooded yearly, leaving behind nutrient-rich silt. This silt helped farmers produce abundant crops, but unpredictable floods could also wipe out fields and settlements. As a result, ancient Chinese communities developed sophisticated methods to control water, including building dikes, canals, and irrigation systems. Over many generations, these efforts supported larger populations and more elaborate food production methods.

Northern China (around the Yellow River) had a cooler, drier climate, making it suitable for growing **millet** and later **wheat**. **Millet** was one of the first domesticated grains in this region, offering a hardy and relatively drought-resistant crop that suited the local environment. Over time, wheat (introduced from Western Asia) gained importance, eventually surpassing millet in some areas. But for a long period, millet remained a key staple grain in the north.

Southern China (around and south of the Yangtze River) was warm and more humid. This climate, combined with river-fed fields, allowed for the **cultivation of rice**. Early forms of rice agriculture began along the lower Yangtze centuries ago, gradually spreading throughout the south. In time, rice would become the central staple for much of China, but in the earliest days, its reach was mostly in southern and central regions.

Early Domestication of Plants and Animals

Archaeological sites like **Banpo** and others along the Yellow River show evidence of **millet-based** farming as far back as 6,000–7,000 years ago. These communities lived in semi-subterranean houses, used pottery to cook and store food, and farmed small plots of land. In southern China, sites such as **Hemudu** provide some of the earliest evidence of **rice cultivation** (roughly 7,000 years ago or more). These people used simple wooden tools and built homes on stilts above wet fields.

Domesticated animals played a big role in ancient Chinese diets:

- **Pigs**: One of the earliest and most common domesticated animals, providing meat and fat.

- **Dogs**: Domesticated partly as companions, also potentially used as guard animals or, less commonly, as a food source in certain regions.

- **Chickens**: Became a widespread source of eggs and meat, although the exact timeline of their domestication in China can vary by region.

- **Cattle and Water Buffalo**: Valued for meat, hides, and eventually for plowing (especially in southern rice fields).

- **Sheep and Goats**: More common in the north and western parts of ancient China, where grasslands or steppe areas supported grazing animals.

Early Chinese farmers combined crops and livestock in their communities. They relied on grains for the bulk of their calories, supplemented by vegetables, fruits, and the meat or eggs from domesticated animals. Wild foods—like gathered herbs, nuts, and hunted game—still played a role, especially when harvests were poor.

Regional Differences in Staple Foods

Throughout ancient Chinese history, there was a notable divide between **millet and wheat** in the north and **rice** in the south. Over time, wheat introduced new ways of eating, like making noodles or buns, but in the truly ancient periods, these dishes were not as refined or as widespread as they would become later on. For example, we might see simpler forms of steamed or boiled wheat dough, but not the elaborate noodles of later eras.

In the south, rice was grown in **paddy fields**. Farmers learned to flood these fields to maintain the right moisture for rice plants, controlling weeds and pests more effectively. This required community-wide coordination—digging canals, building levees, and using water buffaloes to plow muddy fields. Because rice fields demanded more labor, southern communities often developed complex social structures to share the workload.

Cooking Methods in Ancient China

Cooking in ancient China involved **boiling, steaming, and roasting**—though the specific techniques varied across regions and time periods. Pottery or bronze vessels might hold grains or stews over a fire. Steaming could be done with bamboo baskets or ceramic containers, especially once those technologies were developed. In the earliest days, clay pots were the main cooking tools, placed directly on or near the fire.

Common dishes included porridges (thin or thick) made from millet or rice, sometimes mixed with bits of vegetables or meat. These porridges, often called **congee** in later times, were very filling and easy to digest. People might season them with salt, if available, or with naturally occurring flavor from bones, wild herbs, or fermented sauces.

Fermentation was an important part of ancient Chinese cooking, even from very early times. Though it was not as advanced as later centuries, the seeds were there: simple **pickled vegetables** or **fermented grains** that could yield early sauces. Some historians believe that the practice of fermenting grains into **wine** (and possibly into a proto soy sauce) started in ancient times. Alcoholic beverages from millet or rice existed at least by the time of the Shang Dynasty (around 1600–1046 BCE).

Societal Organization and Food

Like other ancient regions, China's social structure influenced what people ate. **Nobles and rulers** could afford finer foods—more meat, better grains, and special delicacies brought in from afar. They conducted feasts to show their power, using large bronze vessels to cook and serve food, and offering lavish banquets to their allies or guests. **Common farmers**, on the other hand, ate simpler meals—often millet porridge, vegetables, and occasional meat from pigs or chickens.

The Role of Ritual and Ancestors

In many ancient Chinese cultures, **ancestor worship** was important. People believed that their ancestors, even after death, remained connected to the living family. Food offerings were given at ancestral temples or placed in graves. These offerings included grains, meat, wine, and fruits, symbolizing care and respect for forebears. Archaeologists find bronze ritual vessels in tombs, many bearing inscriptions or designs indicating they were used to prepare or serve special meals.

Ritual meals were central to religious and state ceremonies. Sacrificial offerings might involve slaughtering an animal (like a pig or ox), cooking it, and offering parts of it to spirits or gods. The rest could be consumed in a communal feast, affirming community bonds and social hierarchies.

Early Dynastic Periods and Food

- **Xia Dynasty** (traditionally 2070–1600 BCE, though not well-documented): Believed to be China's first dynasty, it likely practiced the millet- and rice-based agriculture described above. Archaeological sites from this era show pottery, basic bronze tools, and remains of domesticated animals.
- **Shang Dynasty** (1600–1046 BCE): Known for advanced bronze work, including large cooking and serving vessels (dings, guis, etc.). Archaeological evidence suggests the Shang enjoyed banquets featuring meat, grains, and early forms of alcohol. The royal family and nobles had large storehouses for grain and livestock.
- **Zhou Dynasty** (1046–256 BCE): During this time, regional lords governed lands where peasants farmed crops for them. Ritual feasts became even more structured, with etiquette around how and when certain foods and wines were served. Iron tools began to appear in later Zhou times, improving farming efficiency.

By late Zhou, Chinese society was more organized in how it distributed land and managed agriculture. Tools improved, and irrigation methods expanded. The introduction of **iron plows** and more advanced techniques gradually increased crop yields, though that development really started to take off later, beyond our ancient scope.

The Emergence of Rice Culture

While millet remained strong in the north, **rice** increasingly dominated the south. Archaeological findings along the Yangtze River indicate early forms of **wet-rice cultivation**. Flooded fields not only helped rice to grow; they also created habitats for fish, snails, and small crustaceans. Sometimes these were gathered as extra food, showing a **multi-layered** use of the same land.

Rice demanded more labor than millet but could feed more people when grown well. By carefully controlling water flow, southern farmers achieved **double-cropping** in some areas—harvesting rice twice a year. This practice came a bit later but had its roots in ancient experiments with timing and crop rotation. Even in the very early periods, the potential of rice to sustain growing populations was clear.

Foods Beyond the Grains

1. **Vegetables and Fruits**: Ancient Chinese farmers cultivated **leafy greens**, such as early forms of cabbage or mustard greens, along with **root vegetables** like turnips. Native fruits included **peaches** and **plums** (which have a long history in Chinese lore and symbolism), as well as wild berries and melons in some regions.

2. **Legumes**: **Soybeans** may have been domesticated during the Zhou era (or possibly earlier). Although soy products like tofu and soy sauce became widespread in later periods, the ancient beginnings of soybean cultivation laid the groundwork. Other beans and peas were also grown, providing a protein source for many families.

3. **Herbs and Seasonings**: Ginger, green onions, and garlic have deep roots in Chinese cooking. Salt was crucial, sometimes obtained from sea salt pans along the coast or from certain inland salt wells. People learned to make **salted and pickled** vegetables to preserve them for lean times. The famous Chinese five-spice or more complex seasonings developed much later, but the seeds of these ideas were present in the simpler mixes of ancient times.

4. **Meat and Fish**: Beyond pigs and chickens, some areas had **ducks**, **geese**, and even **game** animals like deer or rabbit, caught by hunters. Fish, especially **carp**, thrived in rivers and ponds. In certain regions, fish farming in small ponds began early, improving the local protein supply.

5. **Nuts and Seeds**: People gathered acorns, chestnuts, walnuts, and sesame seeds. Sesame could be pressed for oil or used in cooking. Chestnuts were particularly important in some mountainous regions, roasted or boiled for a sweet, filling treat.

Trade and Exchange

Although ancient China developed mostly on its own in the early stages, there was still some **exchange of ideas and goods** with neighboring peoples. The steppe tribes to the north introduced new livestock breeds or hardy grains. Trade routes along the edge of the deserts might have brought exotic items like jade or certain spices. These exchanges were limited compared to later periods (such as the Silk Road era), but they still influenced local diets and farming practices.

Food and Social Rituals

From early times, food was used to express respect, status, and connection. Hosts were expected to provide their best grains, meats, and possibly wine when entertaining guests. **Banquets** among nobles or at the king's court featured elaborate serving vessels, each with its own ceremonial role. The shape and decoration of bronze vessels often indicated the type of food or drink they contained—some for meats, others for grains, and others for wine.

Feasting also had a **political** aspect. Powerful rulers used lavish meals to impress or reward allies, forging relationships that could lead to support in wars or alliances in trade. People recorded these events on bones, shells, or bronze inscriptions, many of which survive to give us a window into their dining customs.

CHAPTER 8

Indus Valley and Early Indian Cuisine

When we talk about the earliest civilizations in the Indian subcontinent, the **Indus Valley Civilization** stands out. Also called the **Harappan Civilization**, it flourished along the Indus River and its tributaries in what is now Pakistan and parts of northwestern India. At its height (around 2600–1900 BCE), this civilization boasted carefully planned cities with advanced drainage systems, baked brick houses, and a strong agricultural economy. Its people relied on the fertile river plains to grow crops like wheat, barley, and legumes. In this chapter, we will explore what we know about **food in the Indus Valley** and how early Indian cuisine took shape in the centuries that followed.

Geography of the Indus Valley

The Indus River begins in the Himalayas and flows southwest into the Arabian Sea. Along its path, it picks up **silt** that makes nearby land fertile. The Indus Valley region also includes other rivers like the Ravi, Chenab, and Sutlej. These waterways allowed the growth of large urban centers such as **Harappa** and **Mohenjo-daro**, along with smaller towns and villages. Seasonal flooding was vital for farming, although controlling those waters required organization and planning.

Beyond the river plains, the civilization also stretched into drier regions, where farming was more challenging. It is believed that the Indus people built irrigation canals and storage reservoirs to manage water. The large-scale coordination needed for these projects suggests a central authority or cooperation among communities.

Domesticated Crops and Farming Practices

Archaeologists find evidence of **wheat, barley, peas, lentils, chickpeas, and sesame seeds** at Indus Valley sites. Some form of **cotton** was grown too, though that was more for textiles than for food. There is also evidence of **dates**, which might have been cultivated or gathered from palm groves along riverbanks. The climate and soil conditions in certain parts of the Indus region supported these crops well.

Wheat and **barley** were likely turned into breads or porridges. Grinding stones (similar to those found in other ancient cultures) have been uncovered, indicating that people made flour. **Sesame** could be pressed for oil or used as a flavoring. **Chickpeas** and other legumes provided protein, especially for those who could not afford regular meat.

Farming in the Indus Valley may have used **oxen or water buffalo** to pull simple wooden plows. Terracotta models of plows have been discovered, suggesting their importance. Fields would have been carefully laid out, with channels to bring water from rivers or wells. The civilization's ability to produce surplus crops likely supported its sizable urban populations.

Animal Husbandry and Protein Sources

Like other early civilizations, the Indus people domesticated a variety of animals:

- **Cattle** (including water buffalo) for milk, meat, and as draft animals.

- **Sheep and goats** for meat, wool, and milk.

- **Pigs** in some areas, though less commonly mentioned in Indus contexts than in China.

- **Fowl** such as ducks or chickens might have been kept in some places, but solid evidence for domesticated chickens in the Indus region is debated; they may have arrived or become common slightly later.

Hunting likely supplemented the diet. Remains of fish bones and riverine creatures hint that people fished in the Indus and other waterways. The rivers teemed with species that could be smoked, dried, or cooked fresh. Some communities near the coast could also harvest shellfish.

There is limited direct evidence of **dairy products**, but given the presence of cattle, it is plausible that **milk**, **curd**, or **ghee** (clarified butter) might have been part of the diet. These items would be difficult to preserve in the archaeological record, so we rely on indirect clues such as terracotta artifacts shaped like churns or references from later Vedic texts.

Urban Life and Food Distribution

The large cities of **Harappa** and **Mohenjo-daro** were home to tens of thousands of people. They featured **grid-like street plans**, **drainage systems**, and **public wells**. Granaries or large storage buildings have been identified, suggesting that grain was collected and possibly distributed by some form of organized authority. These structures may have helped buffer the population against famine or controlled the flow of goods for trade.

Markets might have existed, where farmers from the countryside brought produce to sell or barter. City dwellers who specialized in crafts—like pottery, metallurgy, or bead-making—relied on these markets for their daily food. Though we do not have written records like Mesopotamian cuneiform or Egyptian hieroglyphs to detail exact transactions, the layout of certain areas in Indus cities hints at commercial activity.

Cooking Tools and Methods in the Indus Valley

Archaeologists uncover **terracotta cooking pots**, **grinding stones**, and **hearths**. Some homes had small raised platforms or simple ovens, where families could bake or roast food. **Clay ovens** might have resembled early tandoor-like structures, though the classic tandoor we think of today likely developed later. Still, the concept of a clay oven for baking flatbreads or roasting meats seems plausible.

Cooking methods likely included:

- **Boiling or stewing** grains and legumes in terracotta pots.

- **Baking breads** made from wheat or barley flour, perhaps shaped into flatbreads and stuck to the walls of a hot clay oven or placed on flat stones over a fire.

- **Roasting or grilling** small cuts of meat or fish over open flames.

- **Drying or smoking** fish and meat to preserve them in a hot climate.

Seasonings might have included **salt**, **herbs**, and possibly **spices** like turmeric or cumin if they were available locally. We cannot be certain which spices they used, but the Indian subcontinent is known for its native spices and aromatic plants. Some seeds or dried leaves might have been added to dishes to enhance flavor. However, chili peppers (a key spice in modern Indian cuisine) only arrived much later from the Americas, so they would not be part of the ancient Indus diet.

Trade and Cultural Exchange

One striking feature of the Indus Valley Civilization was its **trade connections** with Mesopotamia and other regions. Seals with Indus inscriptions have been found in Mesopotamia, and Mesopotamian records mention a land called **"Meluhha,"** which could refer to the Indus region. They likely exchanged goods like **cotton textiles, beads, and perhaps grain or spices**.

This interaction might have influenced food. People in the Indus region could import or learn about Mesopotamian barley varieties, and in turn, Mesopotamians might have received Indus crops or cooking ideas. Overland routes through Iran or maritime routes across the Arabian Sea facilitated such trade. The extent to which this affected daily meals remains partly speculative, but cross-cultural links are clear.

Religious or Ritual Aspects of Food

While we do not have extensive written records of Indus religion, artifacts suggest some form of **ritual practices** involving figurines, seals, and possible shrines. Food offerings to deities or ancestors might have been common, similar to other ancient civilizations. Large communal gatherings could have included feasting, either to celebrate harvest times or honor local gods. Terracotta figurines of bulls or female deities might hint at the significance of fertility—of crops, livestock, and people.

Later Vedic traditions (after the Indus Valley Civilization declined) placed importance on **yajnas** (fire sacrifices), using ghee, grains, and soma (a ritual drink) as offerings. While these texts come from a period somewhat later than the Harappan peak, the concept of ritual offerings likely has deep roots in the subcontinent's ancient cultures.

Post–Indus Valley Transition and Early Indian Cuisine

The Indus Valley Civilization began to wane around 1900 BCE, possibly due to changes in river patterns, climate shifts, or other social factors. Some people migrated eastward or southward, merging with local populations. As new groups, often called **Indo-Aryans**, moved into the northern plains of the subcontinent, different language and cultural practices emerged, forming the basis of **Vedic** civilization.

With time, these groups developed new social structures, including the early beginnings of what would become the caste system. **Cattle** gained religious importance, particularly in Vedic traditions, which influenced how people viewed the consumption of beef. Grains like wheat and barley persisted, while **rice** became more widespread in the Gangetic plains to the east, where rainfall was high.

Although the transition from the Harappan to the Vedic period is still somewhat mysterious, it is clear that **farming** continued to be the bedrock of society. People carried forward knowledge of irrigation and crop management, refining techniques based on local conditions. Over time, new dishes and cooking methods emerged, shaped by these cultural exchanges and innovations.

Diet and Daily Meals in Early Indian Tradition

Following the Indus era, in the broad region of early northern India:

- **Wheat and barley** breads or porridges remained common.

- **Rice** took on a bigger role, especially in eastern or more humid regions, eventually leading to a variety of rice-based dishes.

- **Legumes** like lentils, peas, and chickpeas continued to be vital sources of protein.
- **Dairy** from cows and buffaloes, especially milk and ghee, gained a special place in daily use and ritual contexts.

- **Fruits and vegetables** such as melons, cucumbers, leafy greens, and gourds were grown.

- **Spices and herbs** like coriander, cumin, turmeric, mustard seeds, and ginger began to find their way into everyday cooking, though the full range of Indian spices we know today was not yet present.

Cooking utensils and methods would have been simple but effective—clay or metal pots for boiling or stewing, flat stones or clay plates for baking breads, and open fires or clay ovens for roasting. The **tawa**, a flat or slightly curved pan used later for breads like rotis, might have an ancient predecessor in simple clay or metal disks.

Social Organization and Feasting

Just like Mesopotamia, Egypt, or China, the Indus Valley and later early Indian societies had **social hierarchies** that reflected in their diets. **Wealthier individuals** could afford more variety, including additional spices, clarified butter, and better cuts of meat. **Common farmers** ate simpler meals based on staple grains and legumes, occasionally adding small amounts of meat or dairy products.

Feasts took place during **religious festivals, marriages, harvest celebrations**, or important community gatherings. People likely prepared large communal meals, featuring grains cooked in big pots, vegetable dishes spiced with local herbs, and possibly sweet treats made from milk and honey (if available). These events reinforced social bonds and allowed for cultural traditions to flourish.

Urban-Rural Connections

During the peak of the Indus Valley Civilization, the links between **cities** and **villages** were essential. Farmers in the countryside produced food, some of which was sent to the urban centers. City dwellers specialized in crafts like pottery, jewelry making, or metalwork. This cooperation maintained a balanced economic system, allowing the civilization to endure for centuries.

When the Indus Civilization declined, many of its urban centers were abandoned or shrank. People returned to more **rural lifestyles**, spreading out across the plains. Over time, **new urban centers** arose in the **Gangetic region**, fueled by rice cultivation and evolving cultural practices. The knowledge of farming, livestock breeding, and cooking methods passed down through generations, blending with the traditions of incoming or neighboring groups.

Legacy of the Indus Valley and Early Indian Food Practices

Although the **Indus script** remains largely undeciphered, the civilization's influence can be felt in the agricultural foundations, urban planning concepts, and potential trade networks that shaped South Asia. After the Indus decline, as the Vedic age dawned, many elements of Harappan agricultural and cooking knowledge likely merged with new cultural ideas. Over centuries, these mixes set the stage for the rich **Indian culinary traditions** that would fully blossom in later eras.

Key legacies include:

1. **Advanced irrigation** and water management practices, which future societies built upon.

2. A strong **grain-legume** combination, forming the basis of a balanced diet across social classes.

3. The concept of **urban grain storage** and distribution systems, important for managing surpluses and supporting large populations.

4. Early hints of **spice usage** and possibly some of the cooking techniques that would evolve into recognizable Indian dishes later on.

In the chapters ahead, as we continue our historical journey, we will see how different civilizations around the world refined their farming, cooking, and food customs. The seeds planted by the Indus people and early Vedic cultures would continue to grow into one of the world's most diverse culinary traditions. But before we move further into other parts of Asia or return to the West, we will explore the food worlds of **Ancient Greece** and **the Roman Empire**, where new twists on bread, olive oil, and wine awaited.

CHAPTER 9

Food in Ancient Greece

Ancient Greece was made up of city-states spread across the Greek mainland, the islands of the Aegean Sea, and the western coast of Asia Minor (modern-day Turkey). Famous city-states included **Athens**, **Sparta**, **Corinth**, and **Thebes**. Despite sharing language and many cultural practices, each city-state had its own customs, including those related to food. In this chapter, we explore the main foods, cooking methods, and social practices around meals in Ancient Greece, focusing on the eras before the rise of the Roman Empire.

Geography and Climate: A Basis for Greek Food

Greece's landscape is **mountainous** and **rocky**, with a long coastline. The climate is typically **Mediterranean**, meaning hot, dry summers and mild, wet winters. This environment influenced what crops could grow successfully. The three main pillars of the ancient Greek diet are often said to be:

1. **Grains** (especially barley and wheat)

2. **Olives** (for oil)

3. **Grapes** (for wine)

These pillars shaped the daily meals and economy of Ancient Greece, though many other foods appeared in the Greek diet as well.

Farms in Greece were often small, terraced plots on hillside slopes or narrow coastal plains. Farmers took advantage of every patch of fertile soil. Irrigation was less extensive than in ancient river civilizations like Egypt or Mesopotamia, but Greeks learned to store water and dig small channels where needed. Rainfall during winter months was crucial for growing grains and other crops.

Staple Crops and Basic Diet

Grains: In early Greece, **barley** was more common than wheat because it tolerated the rugged conditions better. Wheat grew well in some regions but often required more fertile land. Both barley and wheat were turned into **bread**, often in the form of flat loaves or small rolls. Athenians, for instance, might eat bread made from barley meal daily, dipping it in wine or olive oil to soften it.

Olive Oil: Olives thrived in rocky, dry soils and became a signature crop of the Greeks. **Olive oil** was used for cooking, for lamp fuel, as a base for perfumes, and in religious ceremonies. Extracting oil involved pressing the olives—initially with simple stone presses. Over time, more sophisticated presses appeared in different regions of Greece.

Wine and Grapes: Grapevines did well on Greek hillsides. Harvested grapes were often **crushed** in large vats, then the juice was placed in containers to **ferment** into wine. Wine came in various qualities and types. Wealthier households had finer wines, sometimes aged or flavored with herbs, while ordinary people drank simpler table wine, often **diluted with water** at mealtimes.

Other Important Foods

1. **Legumes:** Lentils, chickpeas, fava beans, and peas added protein to meals. These could be boiled into soups or mashed into pastes.

2. **Fruits and Vegetables:** Grapes (beyond wine) were eaten fresh or dried into raisins. Figs, apples, and pomegranates were common fruits. Vegetables like cabbages, onions, and garlic appeared in many dishes. Cucumbers, leeks, and lettuce grew well in gardens.

3. **Cheese and Dairy:** Goats and sheep were the main livestock in Greece's hilly terrain. Their **milk** could be made into cheese or yogurt-like products. **Feta-like cheeses** from sheep or goat milk might have early origins in this time, though exact names and recipes varied.

4. **Fish and Seafood:** With so much coastline, fish and seafood played a big role in the Greek diet, especially in coastal city-states. Fish could be **grilled**, **salted**, or **dried**. Octopus, squid, and shellfish were also eaten. Wealthy people often enjoyed fresh fish from the market, while salted or dried fish could be transported farther inland.

5. **Meat:** Greeks did eat meat—mainly goat, sheep, and sometimes pork. Beef or oxen were rarer, often used in **religious sacrifices** or for wealthier banquets. Hunting brought in wild boar or deer, though this was more common in rural areas. Poultry (chickens, geese, ducks) offered eggs and meat, but they were not as central as in later European diets.

Cooking Methods and Common Dishes

Greeks typically cooked with **clay pots** and **open hearths**. Ovens might be communal or at least simple dome-shaped structures at home. **Boiling, roasting, and stewing** were frequent methods. Frying required a generous use of precious olive oil, so it was less common than in modern times.

Popular Preparations:

- **Bread and Porridge**: Barley could be ground into meal and boiled into a thick porridge called **maza**. This might be eaten as is, or formed into small loaves when mixed with water, yeast, or sourdough starter.

- **Soups and Stews**: Legume soups, seasoned with onions or herbs, formed hearty meals for many Greeks. Meats could be boiled into stews, often with vegetables and bits of bread to thicken the broth.

- **Fish Dishes**: A fish might be **roasted** over a fire, brushed with oil and herbs, or boiled in a pot with onions, greens, and sometimes wine.

- **Cheese and Honey Pairings**: Cheese, especially goat cheese, paired well with **honey** for sweeter snacks. Honey was the main sweetener in Ancient Greece, used both in desserts and in sweet-sour sauces for meats or fish.

Seasonings included **salt**, **olive oil**, **vinegar**, **herbs** (like oregano, thyme, rosemary), and occasionally **garum-like fish sauces** introduced from or influenced by other Mediterranean cultures. Spices such as pepper were very expensive imports, so they were used sparingly by the wealthiest classes, if at all.

Social Customs Around Food: The Symposium and the Daily Meal

Ancient Greeks generally ate **three main meals** a day:

1. **Breakfast (akratisma)**: Often just barley bread dipped in wine, sometimes with figs or olives.

2. **Midday Meal (ariston)**: A light meal that might include bread, cheese, and perhaps some fish or vegetables.

3. **Evening Meal (deipnon)**: The main meal of the day, more elaborate with multiple dishes. Families gathered together, and it could include friends or neighbors as guests.

Among wealthier Greeks, a separate gathering called the **symposium** followed the evening meal. A symposium was a social event where men (often excluding women, except for entertainers or special guests) reclined on couches and drank wine mixed with water, discussing politics, philosophy, or sharing poetry. **Food at a symposium** was mostly small snacks or sweets, as the main meal had already been eaten. This gathering was as much about conversation and entertainment as it was about eating.

Feasts, Celebrations, and Religious Contexts

Religious festivals were a major part of Greek life. Many city-states had patron gods or goddesses, and they celebrated with public feasts or processions. **Sacrificial meats**—from goats, sheep, or oxen—were offered to the gods at temples, with parts of the animal burned as an offering. The remaining meat might be cooked and shared among participants, uniting the community in a ritual meal.

One famous festival in Athens was the **Panathenaea**, honoring Athena. While the festival included sports and processions, a highlight was the offering of a **sacrificial cow** (and sometimes more) at the Acropolis. After the sacrifice, people enjoyed the meat in a grand communal feast.

Household worship also occurred, with smaller offerings of bread, wine, or fruit placed on altars for the family's chosen deities. Some families might thank the gods for a good harvest or a successful fishing trip by dedicating the first share of their meal.

Markets and Trade in Ancient Greece

Each city-state, or **polis**, had a central market area called the **agora** (in Athens, the Athenian Agora was famous). People went there to buy or sell fresh produce, fish, meat, pottery, and other goods. Farmers from the countryside brought crops early in the morning. Fishermen arrived with the catch of the day—some fish still alive in baskets of water.

Greek city-states also traded with each other and with foreign lands. They exported **olive oil, wine, pottery, and metalwork**, sometimes receiving **grain** from regions like the Black Sea coast, where farmland was more plentiful. Spices, luxury items, and exotic foods could arrive via ships from Egypt, Phoenicia, or other parts of the Mediterranean. While these goods were expensive, they enriched the diets and cooking methods of wealthier Greeks who could afford them.

The Diet of Spartan Warriors vs. Athenian Citizens

Sparta, known for its strict military culture, had different attitudes toward food than Athens. Young Spartan males lived in communal barracks and ate the infamous **"black broth,"** a soup made with pork, vinegar, salt, and possibly blood. This was considered a simple, hearty meal to sustain warriors without indulging in luxury. In contrast, Athenians enjoyed a wider variety of foods and flavors, priding themselves on refined banquets and symposia.

Despite the differences, both city-states relied on the same core crops (grains, olives, grapes) and shared many similar cooking techniques. Yet Spartan culture dictated more austere meals, reflecting their emphasis on discipline and military readiness. Athenians, with a strong cultural focus on **art, drama, and philosophy**, spent more time on culinary pleasures and social dining experiences.

Health and Diet in Ancient Greece

Greek thinkers took an interest in food's effect on **health** and **balance** in the body. Early physicians, like Hippocrates, wrote about the importance of a moderate diet. They believed that certain foods could heat or cool the body, dry or moisten it, aligning with the four humors (blood, phlegm, yellow bile, black bile). While more detailed humoral theory emerged later, the seeds of this approach can be seen in how Greeks viewed balance in meals.

Foods like **barley porridge** were considered nourishing and easy to digest. Vegetables like onions and garlic were believed to have medicinal properties. **Wine**, when diluted and consumed in moderation, was viewed as healthy, but drinking it undiluted or to excess was frowned upon. Olive oil was considered a healthy source of fat. The emphasis on balance and moderation influenced Greek cuisine for centuries, even beyond the classical period.

Women and Food in Ancient Greece

In many Greek city-states, women oversaw household food tasks—grinding grain, baking bread, cooking daily meals. **Wealthier families** might have enslaved persons or hired cooks, but women still played a central role in managing supplies and deciding daily menus. However, in public spheres, like the symposium, it was typically men who took center stage. Women's involvement in formal banquets was limited, except in certain religious festivals or if they were part of the entertainment (e.g., flute girls or dancers).

This dynamic meant that women's knowledge of cooking, food preservation, and flavoring was highly valued within the home but less recognized in public. Recipes and cooking secrets were often passed from mother to daughter informally, with no official written guides (at least, very few have survived).

Influence of Greek Food Culture on Neighboring Regions

Greek colonists established settlements around the Mediterranean and Black Sea, bringing with them Greek agriculture (olive trees, grapevines), cooking styles, and social dining customs. Over time, local populations blended Greek ways with their own. Meanwhile, Greeks also adopted some native foods from these regions, broadening their culinary repertoire.

Traders from **Phoenicia**, **Egypt**, and **Asia Minor** influenced Greek diets, introducing new fruits, spices, and cooking techniques. For example, Greek cooks might experiment with more elaborate sauces after tasting Phoenician or Eastern dishes. Although many details are lost to history, it is clear that food in ancient Greece was never isolated; it evolved through contact with many cultures, setting a precedent for future Mediterranean cuisine.

CHAPTER 10

The Roman Empire and Its Feasts

The **Roman Empire** grew from a small city on the Tiber River to control vast territories around the Mediterranean Sea and beyond. At its height, it encompassed modern-day Italy, Spain, France (Gaul), Greece, parts of the Middle East, North Africa, and even Britain. Over centuries, Rome's power and wealth shaped a distinct culinary tradition that blended local Italian foods with influences from conquered or allied regions. From simple peasant fare to lavish banquets in marble villas, Roman food culture was diverse, inventive, and sometimes extravagant. In this chapter, we explore how Romans sourced, cooked, and consumed their meals—focusing on the era of the Republic and the early Empire, before major changes brought by later medieval times.

The Setting: From Republic to Empire

Rome began as a small settlement in central Italy, traditionally dated to 753 BCE. Over time, it transformed into a **Republic**, then eventually an **Empire** under emperors like **Augustus** (starting in 27 BCE). During these centuries, Rome's expansion introduced new tastes, ingredients, and cooking methods. Conquered territories paid taxes and sent shipments of grain, oil, wine, and spices to feed Rome's growing population.

The city of **Rome** itself became a massive metropolis, with hundreds of thousands (eventually over a million) residents. Feeding such a large population required organized trade routes, extensive farming estates, and clever storage solutions like **granaries**. Wealthy Romans developed **latifundia**—large estates that mass-produced crops such as grains, olives, and grapes. Meanwhile, smaller farms still existed, supplying local markets with fresh produce, meat, and dairy.

Roman Staples: Grain, Wine, and Oil

Grain (especially wheat) was at the heart of Rome's diet, replaced older staples like barley for much of the population. Wheat was milled into **flour** for bread, or boiled into porridge (puls). The Roman government sometimes **subsidized grain** (later offering free bread) to keep urban poor fed and reduce the risk of unrest. By the Imperial period, wheat imports arrived from provinces like Egypt and North Africa, ensuring a steady supply.

Wine was consumed by all social classes, although quality varied widely. Fine wines came from regions like **Campania** (near Naples) or **Falernian** wine from the slopes of Mount Falernus. Common folk drank cheaper table wine. Romans, like the Greeks, often **diluted** their wine with water. They sometimes flavored it with herbs, honey, or spices, creating beverages like **mulsum** (honey wine).

Olive Oil was vital for cooking, lighting lamps, and making soap-like cleaning products. Italy's climate, especially in regions like **Apulia** and **Calabria**, supported vast olive groves. Over time, the Empire also drew oil from provinces like Hispania (Spain) and Africa Proconsularis (Tunisia). Amphorae filled with olive oil traveled by ship or wagon to reach city markets.

Other Key Foods in Ancient Rome

1. **Bread and Baked Goods**: Roman bakers developed a wide range of breads, from **simple loaves** to **finer breads** using sifted flour. Public bakeries employed kneading machines driven by animals. Some loaves were shaped into circular rounds with dividing lines for easy breaking.
2. **Puls (Porridge)**: In early Republican Rome, puls (a thick grain porridge) was a staple for peasants and soldiers. Over time, bread replaced puls as the main grain dish in wealthier households, but it remained a common food among the lower classes.
3. **Vegetables and Legumes**: Romans ate onions, leeks, garlic, cabbages, lettuce, turnips, beans, lentils, chickpeas, and more. Cabbage, in particular, was considered healthy, sometimes eaten raw or boiled.
4. **Fruits**: Apples, pears, grapes, figs, dates, cherries, plums, and quinces were common, depending on the region and season. Wealthy Romans had orchards on their estates or purchased fruit from specialized sellers. **Figs and grapes** could be dried for year-round consumption.

5. **Meat and Poultry**: Common meats included pork, beef, lamb, goat, and game (e.g., hare, boar, deer). Romans also raised chickens, geese, and ducks for eggs and meat. Wild birds like thrushes might appear on high-end tables. However, many ordinary people ate meat rarely, except on special occasions.

6. **Fish and Seafood**: Fish was popular along coastal areas. Seafood like oysters, mussels, and octopus could be served at elite banquets. Romans also developed **fish farms**—piscinae—for raising species such as carp or mullet. Salted fish and **garum**, a fermented fish sauce, became widely used condiments.

7. **Cheese and Dairy**: Romans produced **cheese** from sheep, goat, and cow milk. **Ricotta-like** and **hard cheeses** existed. Milk was also used to make simple puddings or combined with eggs for custard-like dishes.

Seasonings and Sauces: The Love for Garum

Romans were known for their **bold flavors**, especially in the Imperial era. A key condiment was **garum** (or liquamen), made by fermenting fish (like anchovies) with salt over weeks or months. The resulting liquid was salty, savory, and rich in **umami**. It was drizzled over meats, mixed with wine or vinegar, and even used in sweet dishes with honey. Different grades of garum, some extremely expensive, were traded across the Empire.

Other seasonings included:

- **Salt**: Often mined or evaporated from seawater.

- **Vinegar**: Made from sour wine, used in cooking and as a refreshing drink (posca) when mixed with water.

- **Herbs**: Oregano, thyme, mint, rosemary, and bay leaves.

- **Imported Spices**: Pepper, cinnamon, ginger, and others from Asia. These were luxury items, mostly reserved for the wealthy.

- **Honey**: The main sweetener. Rome lacked sugar, so honey sweetened dishes, drinks, and desserts.

Roman Meals: From Peasant Fare to Lavish Banquets

Romans typically ate **three main meals**:

1. **Ientaculum** (Breakfast): Often a light meal—bread dipped in wine or cheese, perhaps olives or dried fruit. Poorer Romans might skip or have a very simple breakfast.

2. **Prandium** (Midday Meal): Another quick meal of leftovers, bread, fruit, or cold meats from the previous day if available. Some might have a small dish of vegetables or salted fish.

3. **Cena** (Main Evening Meal): In early Republican times, cena took place in mid-afternoon. But by the late Republic and Imperial eras, it shifted to later in the evening and grew more elaborate, especially for the wealthy.

For wealthy households, the cena could be a grand affair with multiple courses:

- **Gustatio (Appetizers)**: Light dishes to whet the appetite, like eggs, salads, oysters, or salted fish. Often served with a sweet-and-sour sauce or dipped in garum.

- **Prima Mensa (Main Courses)**: Roasted or boiled meats, fish, vegetables, heavily spiced stews, all served with bread and wine.

- **Secunda Mensa (Desserts)**: Fruits, sweet pastries, or honey-based confections. Some wealthy banquets featured exotic offerings like stuffed dormice or flamingo tongues, mostly to show status.

Guests **reclined** on couches around a **triclinum** (dining table) arranged in a U-shape, with servants bringing each course. Conversation, entertainment (musicians, dancers, or readings from literature), and sometimes even debates occurred during the meal. The host's goal was to impress visitors with the variety and abundance of dishes.

For **poorer Romans**, cena was simpler: a bowl of vegetable soup or porridge, bread, some olives, maybe a piece of cheese or salted fish. Meat or fresh fish were rare treats. They might buy hot snacks from street vendors if they had a bit of extra money.

Feasting Culture: Status and Display

Roman banquets often served as a stage to **show off wealth**, form **political alliances**, or reward **supporters**. **Patrons** invited **clients** to dinner, building loyalty through generosity. Emperors and senators used lavish feasts to demonstrate power. Large villas had separate kitchens, storerooms, and staff to handle cooking. Detailed **cookbooks**, like the one attributed to **Apicius** (though compiled over time), described complex recipes using expensive ingredients.

Exotic foods—like peacock, ostrich, or imported spices—symbolized the host's wealth. Live entertainment (acrobats, poets, or musicians) spiced up the event. Drinking could be heavy, though respectable Romans prided themselves on controlling drunkenness, at least in theory.

Roman Markets and Trade Routes

Rome's location in the **center of the Mediterranean** allowed it to integrate trade from three continents: Europe, Africa, and Asia. **Trade routes** by sea and land connected major ports, linking the Empire in a vast economic network. Grain from Egypt, Africa, and Sicily fed Rome; wine and oil traveled from Spain and southern Gaul; spices arrived overland from Asia or by ship from the Red Sea.

In urban centers, large **public markets** sold fresh produce, meats, and fish. Bakers, butchers, and specialized shops lined busy streets. Some neighborhoods had communal **mill-bakeries** where families could bring wheat to be ground and baked into bread. Street vendors and thermopolia (like ancient snack bars) offered quick meals—stews, mulled wine, or fried pastries—to passersby. This vibrant marketplace culture gave many city dwellers variety in daily meals, depending on what they could afford.

Food Preservation and Storage

Preservation was crucial. Romans used several methods:

- **Salting and Drying**: Meat and fish were heavily salted and air-dried to prevent spoilage. Salted fish was especially popular in coastal areas.

- **Pickling**: Vegetables and fruits were pickled in vinegar or brine.

- **Smoking**: Some meats or cheeses could be smoked to extend shelf life.

- **Cellars and Grain Silos**: Large estates and city granaries stored wheat or barley for months or years.

- **Amphorae**: Wine, oil, and sauces (like garum) were sealed in clay amphorae. Beeswax or resin might line the inside to help preserve liquids.

These methods allowed Romans to move goods across great distances, supplying legionnaires on remote frontiers or shipping delicacies to the capital.

The Role of Slavery in Roman Food Production

A significant portion of Roman agriculture and cooking labor came from **enslaved people**. Large estates often employed hundreds of enslaved workers to tend fields, orchards, and livestock. Wealthy households had enslaved cooks, servers, and household managers. This system enabled the lavish lifestyles of the upper classes. For these workers, life was harsh, and though skilled cooks could gain some respect, they remained under the control of their owners.

Regional Variations in the Roman Empire

Rome's vast territory meant **local cuisines** differed widely:

- **Italy**: Focused on wheat bread, olive oil, wine, pork, and vegetables like cabbage and beans.
- **Gaul (France)**: Abundant dairy, with cheeses and butter more common. Wine also produced in regions like Bordeaux.
- **Hispania (Spain)**: Large olive groves, vineyards, and some of the best garum factories along the coast (e.g., in Baetica).
- **North Africa**: Supplied huge amounts of grain and olive oil, along with fruits like figs and dates.
- **Eastern Mediterranean**: Strong Greek influences, advanced seafood dishes, complex bread-making, more spices from Asian trade routes.
- **Britannia (Britain)**: Adapted Roman crops to cooler climates, with barley, wheat, and animals like pigs and sheep. Less wine-growing, so imported more of it.

These regions fed into a shared Roman identity, but each had distinct local favorites. Soldiers and travelers carried cooking ideas across the Empire, leading to a fusion of tastes.

Decline and Transition

Over time, the Western Roman Empire faced economic troubles, invasions, and internal strife. By the 5th century CE, the western part of the Empire fractured, though the Eastern Roman Empire (Byzantine Empire) persisted. Gradually, trade routes weakened in the West, large estates broke up, and the grand banquets of classical Rome faded. Yet many Roman food practices—like bread-making, wine production, and the use of certain sauces—survived, blending into the emerging medieval European cultures.

Lasting Influence of Roman Cuisine

Roman culinary ideas lived on through **written texts**, **archeological finds**, and the continuing traditions of former Roman lands. The **Mediterranean triad** of grain, wine, and oil remained key in southern Europe for centuries. Roman roads and trade links also paved the way for cultural exchange, meaning dishes spread farther than ever before. The emphasis on **social dining**, elaborate courses, and the symbolic power of banquets influenced later European courts.

The famous **cookbook "Apicius"** (though compiled over a few centuries) preserves a snapshot of high-end Roman cooking—featuring garum, exotic spices, and complex combinations of sweet, sour, and savory flavors. This text offers a valuable look at the creativity and tastes of Rome's elite. Meanwhile, everyday Romans taught Europe about simpler bread baking, cheese-making, orchard management, and the value of a hearty stew.

With the fall of Rome in the west, new powers rose. Germanic kingdoms, the Byzantine Empire in the east, and eventually the Islamic Caliphates in the south each carried forward or adapted Roman food traditions in different ways. But as we close this chapter, we have a sense of how the Roman Empire shaped the ancient world's food scene—spreading grains, sauces, and cooking styles across multiple continents.

CHAPTER 11

Food in Medieval Europe

When we say "Medieval Europe," we are talking about a long span of time after the fall of the Western Roman Empire (around the 5th century) up to roughly the late 15th century. During these centuries, Europe went through many changes in leadership, religion, and social order. Feudalism became a common way to organize society, with kings, nobles, knights, and peasants all playing different roles. This structure affected how food was produced, shared, and consumed.

In this chapter, we will see how life on manors, the influence of the Church, and local traditions shaped the way Medieval Europeans grew and prepared their meals. We will also learn about common dishes, drinks, cooking methods, and the important differences between the diets of the rich and the poor.

Feudalism and the Manor System

In many parts of Medieval Europe, people lived under **feudalism**, which was a system of obligations and loyalty. A **king** might grant land to **nobles** or **lords**. These nobles then oversaw **manors**, which included farmland, pastures, a village (or several), and sometimes forests. **Peasants** (often called **serfs** if they were bound to the land) worked the fields, cared for animals, and gave a portion of their harvest to the lord as rent or tax. In return, they got protection and a place to live.

Because of this setup, food production revolved around local farms. Most of what people ate came from the immediate area. Long-distance trade still existed, but it was slower and more expensive. Spices from distant lands were precious luxuries only available to wealthy nobles or royals.

Common Crops and Basic Diets

Medieval Europeans grew **cereals** (grains) like wheat, rye, oats, and barley. Grains were the **main source of calories** for most people, especially peasants. However, the type of grain people ate depended on their wealth and location:

- **Wheat**: Preferred for making the best bread (white bread), usually reserved for the upper classes.

- **Rye** and **Barley**: More common for everyday folk. Bread made from rye or barley was darker and tougher.

- **Oats**: Used for porridge or simple bread in some regions, especially in northern climates.

Besides grains, people grew **vegetables** like onions, leeks, cabbages, and beans. **Legumes** (peas, beans, lentils) were critical as a protein source, especially for those who could not afford much meat. **Root vegetables**, such as turnips and parsnips, were also popular. In some areas, carrots (though often not the bright orange kind we see today) and beets appeared in stews and soups.

Fruit trees lined manor orchards. Apples, pears, plums, and cherries were common in many regions. People ate them fresh in season, or dried them for later. Nuts—like hazelnuts and walnuts—could be gathered from forests, offering extra protein and fats.

Livestock and Meat

Medieval peasants typically raised **pigs**, **sheep**, **goats**, and sometimes a few **cows** for milk. Chickens provided eggs, and occasionally meat. However, meat was not a large part of a peasant's diet. Many peasants only ate meat on special occasions or feast days.

Pigs were relatively easy to feed, as they could roam in forests eating acorns and other scraps. **Sheep** provided wool for clothing and lamb meat. **Cattle** were often used as work animals, pulling plows and carts, though some areas specialized in dairy and cheese-making.

Wealthy nobles, on the other hand, enjoyed **venison** (deer), **boar**, and sometimes exotic meats like swan or peacock. They also hosted hunts in forests, which were strictly protected and reserved for the lord's use—peasants were often forbidden from hunting there. This gave the nobility exclusive access to certain meats.

Cooking Methods

In the peasant's home (often a one-room or two-room hut), there was usually an **open hearth** in the central area. A kettle or pot might hang over the fire to make **pottage**—a thick soup or stew made from grains, vegetables, and sometimes scraps of meat. Bread was baked in village ovens if the manor had one, or on flat stones near the fire.

In the manor house or castle, kitchens were larger, sometimes in a separate building to reduce fire risk. Cooks roasted whole animals on **spits** over big fireplaces and used multiple pots for stews or sauces. They might bake pies in enclosed ovens. **Spices** like cinnamon, ginger, pepper, and cloves—when available—were used to flavor meat dishes or create sweet-sour sauces. These spices were expensive, so using them was a sign of wealth.

Salt was crucial for preserving foods, especially meat and fish. With no modern refrigeration, salting and smoking were common ways to store food for winter or times of scarcity. Fish could also be **dried**, especially in coastal areas or near rivers.

A Typical Day's Meals

- **Breakfast**: Often very simple for peasants—bread, ale or water, perhaps some leftover pottage. Lords might have more variety, like eggs, butter, cheese, or even leftover roasted meats.

- **Midday Meal**: The main meal for peasants, often a thick pottage with bread. If they had access to vegetables from their small plots, they might add onions, cabbage, or beans. For lords, midday could also be a substantial meal with multiple courses.

- **Evening Meal**: Possibly more bread, leftover stew, or soup. In wealthier households, dinner might be grand, featuring roasted meats, sauces, and sweet desserts (like spiced fruit tarts).

Ale or **beer** was common in many parts of northern Europe, even for peasants. Water sources could be dirty, so weak ale or beer was safer to drink. In southern regions (like parts of France or Italy), **wine** might replace ale. But again, the best wines went to the rich. Lower-quality, sour wines or watered-down versions were more accessible to the common folk.

The Role of the Church

Christianity had a profound effect on food in Medieval Europe. **Monasteries** often had large gardens and kept detailed knowledge of farming, herbal medicine, and cheese-making. Monks brewed **ale** or **beer** and sometimes produced **wine** (particularly in areas like France or Germany). Monasteries became local centers of agricultural innovation and food production.

There were also rules around **fasting** and **feast** days. On certain holy days or during Lent, meat was forbidden for most people. They ate fish, eggs, cheese, or simply vegetables and bread. Over time, the Church defined many days of the year as "meatless," shaping how families planned their meals. Fish consumption, especially salted or dried fish, grew as a result.

Feast days—like Christmas, Easter, or the feast of a local saint—allowed for more lavish meals. Even peasants might have better bread, some meat, and perhaps sweet treats if ingredients were available. Lords hosted banquets to show generosity, inviting knights, local officials, and sometimes villagers for big communal meals.

Banquets in Castles

When medieval **lords or kings** held **banquets**, the displays could be quite dramatic. Tables were set in the great hall, often just long boards on trestles. People might **recline** or sit on benches. Wealthy guests ate from **trencher bread** (thick slices of stale bread used like plates) or shared large platters.

Entertainment at these feasts could include **minstrels**, **jugglers**, or even **mock battles**. The food itself was sometimes arranged in fanciful shapes—a peacock roasted and then "re-dressed" in its feathers, or a meat pie with live birds that flew out when cut open (though this was more of a legend than a common reality). Sweet and savory dishes could be mixed, with heavily spiced sauces.

Spice blends were popular: one mixture might include cinnamon, ginger, black pepper, and saffron. Sugar, brought in from distant lands, was very expensive. Honey was also used as a sweetener. Only the highest ranks could afford these luxuries.

Differences Between Rich and Poor

The gap between **rich and poor** was evident in Medieval Europe's food. While nobles dined on roasted meats, pastries, and sweetmeats, peasants mainly ate **coarse bread**, **pottage**, and **seasonal vegetables**. A peasant might taste meat rarely, possibly only during a feast or holiday.

Peasants often faced hunger if crops failed. Famine was a constant threat. They had limited ways to store surplus grain, so a bad harvest meant real hardship. In times of shortage, peasants might turn to wild foods—collecting berries, nuts, mushrooms, or even acorns.

Wealthier families, on the other hand, could survive poor harvests by buying imported grain or stored reserves. They also had more variety: game from forests, fish from stocked ponds, fruit from private orchards, and dairy from large herds.

Town Life and Markets

Though many people lived on **manors** in the countryside, **towns** and **cities** grew in this period, especially from the 11th century onward. Town markets sold fresh produce, bread, meat, fish, and ale. Craftsmen like bakers, butchers, brewers, and tavern keepers became more common.

In bigger trading centers—like **Venice**, **Genoa**, **Cologne**, or **Paris**—wealthy merchants could afford imported goods like dried fruits, spices, or fine wines. Guilds regulated quality and prices. Bakers' guilds, for instance, set rules about how bread should be baked and sold.

City dwellers had access to more foods than peasants on distant manors, but they also faced risks like disease outbreaks due to crowded living conditions. Still, the variety of products in bustling marketplaces offered a glimpse into the changes that would come in later centuries.

Food Preservation and Storage

Salting and smoking meat and fish were crucial. **Pickling** vegetables in brine or vinegar also helped them last longer. **Cheese** was a way to preserve milk, turning a short-lasting liquid into a solid product that could keep for weeks or months. Butter might be made, but it spoiled faster than cheese.

Grain could be stored in barns or **silos**, but it was at risk of moisture, rodents, or mold. If harvests were good, people tried to keep extra grain for next year. But many farmers produced only enough to last through winter, leaving them vulnerable if something went wrong.

In monasteries and some large estates, monks or stewards kept more systematic records, tracking how much grain, cheese, or salted meat was stored. This helped them plan for lean times, though it was not a foolproof system.

Influence of the Church on Specific Foods

We mentioned that certain days required **fasting** or **abstaining** from meat. This led to inventive ways to classify animals. For example, **beavers** or certain waterfowl were sometimes considered "fish" by Church authorities, so they could be eaten on meatless days. Similarly, people developed recipes that looked like meat but used fish or vegetables, bending the rules slightly.

Monastic orders also contributed to brewing and winemaking traditions. Abbey ales and monastic wines gained a reputation for quality, partly because monks had the time and resources to refine their crafts. The Church's calendar of saints' days created frequent feast days, which provided a break from routine and allowed people to celebrate with shared meals.

Herbs and Simple Medicines

Herbs like **parsley, sage, rosemary, thyme, and mint** grew in kitchen gardens, used for both flavor and basic medicinal purposes. The local wise woman or village herbalist might suggest certain herbs for stomach aches or fevers. Monks in monasteries often copied ancient herbal manuscripts, keeping this knowledge alive.

The concept of **"humors"** (blood, phlegm, black bile, yellow bile) continued from ancient Greece and Rome, influencing how doctors recommended diets. For example, if someone had too much "heat," they might be advised to eat cooling foods like certain fruits or leafy greens. Though this was not a strict science, it shaped how some wealthy or educated people chose what to eat.

Changing Food Customs Over Time

By the **High Middle Ages** (around the 11th to 13th centuries), some improvements in farming techniques—like better plows and horse collars—led to higher yields in certain regions. Population grew, and towns expanded. Trade networks got busier, especially in the Mediterranean, bringing more goods and occasional new foods. Spices like **pepper** or **cinnamon** became slightly more common (though still expensive).

In the **Late Middle Ages** (roughly 14th to 15th centuries), Europe faced turmoil from wars and diseases. These events sometimes disrupted farming or trade, causing food shortages or changes in diet. However, by the end of the medieval period, more structured markets had emerged, guilds were well-established, and the seeds of future agricultural and culinary changes were planted.

Overall Legacy of Medieval European Food

Medieval Europe created a foundation for many later cuisines. The **manor system** shaped how land was farmed and how peasants ate. The **Church** guided feast and fast days, encouraging fish consumption and giving monasteries a special role in food production. Towns and trade helped new ingredients reach different regions, though luxuries remained limited to the upper classes.

Although the daily meal of a peasant—dark bread, pottage, and a mug of ale—was far from the fancy banquets of lords, both reflected the broader medieval world: a place of strict social hierarchies, local farming, and strong influence from religious institutions.

CHAPTER 12

Medieval Middle East and the Islamic Golden Age

The **Medieval Middle East** saw the rise of powerful Islamic empires that spanned from the western parts of Asia to North Africa and sometimes into the Iberian Peninsula (southern Spain). The period often called the **Islamic Golden Age** (roughly 8th to 13th centuries) was marked by great advancements in science, medicine, literature, and trade. Major cities like **Baghdad**, **Córdoba**, **Damascus**, and **Cairo** became bustling centers of learning and culture, each with its own culinary traditions.

In this chapter, we discover how these dynasties—particularly under the **Abbasid Caliphate**—shaped food production, cooking techniques, and trade across vast territories. We will see how old influences from the Greeks, Persians, and Romans blended with new ideas, creating a rich tapestry of medieval Middle Eastern cuisine.

The Islamic World Expands: Geography and Trade

After the founding of Islam in the 7th century, Arab armies and traders spread across the Middle East, North Africa, and parts of Asia. By the time of the **Abbasid Caliphate** (established in 750 CE), Baghdad became a major capital, strategically located near the Tigris River. The empire spanned regions that produced a huge variety of foods:

- **Fertile Crescent** areas offered wheat, barley, dates, and vegetables.
- **Egypt** supplied grain from the Nile Delta, along with onions, garlic, and beans.

- **North Africa** contributed olives, fruits, and access to the Mediterranean.

- **Persia** brought sophisticated cooking traditions, including rice dishes and unique spice blends.

- **Al-Andalus** (Muslim-ruled Spain) added new crops like citrus fruits, along with knowledge of irrigation techniques.

Far-reaching **trade routes** connected the Middle East to India, China, sub-Saharan Africa, and even parts of Europe. Caravans traveled across deserts, carrying **spices**, **textiles**, and **luxury foods**, while ships in the Indian Ocean and Mediterranean Sea linked ports. This constant exchange brought exotic ingredients—like cinnamon, nutmeg, saffron, and sugar—to wealthy cities of the Islamic world.

Agriculture and Irrigation

In many Islamic regions, **irrigation** was key. Engineers improved older Persian systems like the **qanat** (underground channels that tapped mountain water). Canals, wells, and water-lifting devices (like the **shaduf** and **noria**) helped farms thrive even in dry environments. Government officials or wealthy landowners often built large estates, growing staples like **wheat**, **barley**, **rice**, and **sugarcane**.

Rice was especially important in Persia and other eastern areas of the caliphate. Over time, it spread to places like Iraq and parts of the Levant. **Sugarcane** cultivation expanded in warm climates, fueling a growing taste for sweet dishes. Cultivation of **citrus fruits**—lemons, oranges, and limes—also flourished, especially in Spain and North Africa, thanks to irrigation and mild climates.

Common Foods and Cooking Methods

Despite regional differences, some staples united the Medieval Middle East:

1. **Grains**: Wheat remained central. It was milled into flour for **flatbreads** (like khubz), round loaves, or sometimes noodles. Barley was used for simple breads or as animal feed.

2. **Rice**: Appeared in various dishes—cooked with spices, meat, or vegetables. Persian-style **pilaf** (or pulao) was a favorite, featuring fragrant rice grains lightly seasoned.

3. **Legumes**: Lentils, chickpeas, and fava beans (ful) were widely consumed in stews, soups, or mashed into dips like **hummus**.

4. **Meat**: Lamb, goat, and chicken were common. Beef was less popular than in Europe, though it was used in some regions. Camel meat was eaten in desert areas. Meat was often roasted, stewed, or grilled on skewers (kebabs).

5. **Fish**: Coastal regions and river cities enjoyed fresh or salted fish. The Arabian Gulf, Red Sea, and Mediterranean all provided seafood.

6. **Dairy**: Sheep or goat milk was made into yogurt or cheese. Yogurt-based sauces and drinks (like ayran) were common, especially in hot climates.

Cooking methods included braising (slow cooking in liquid), grilling, frying, and baking in clay ovens or over open fires. Spices and herbs—cumin, coriander, turmeric, mint, and more—gave dishes their signature aromas. Many recipes combined sweet and savory, mixing fruits or honey with meat and spices. **Sour elements** like vinegar, lemon juice, or sumac balanced flavors.

The Spread of Sugar and Confectionery

Sugar had been known in ancient times (especially in India), but it spread more widely across the Islamic world in the medieval period. Sugarcane plantations flourished in regions like Egypt and Syria, producing **crystal sugar** that replaced honey in some desserts.

Cooks in Baghdad, Damascus, or Córdoba invented **confections** using sugar, nuts (almonds, pistachios), and spices. Simple forms of **halva** or nougat might appear at banquets. Syrups were drizzled over pastries made from thin dough (an early version of **baklava** might date to this era). The sweet tooth of the Islamic Golden Age influenced later European confectionery, as Crusaders and traders returned with tales of sugary delights.

Food and Religion: Islamic Dietary Laws

In the Islamic world, **religious guidelines** affected what people ate:

1. **Halal**: Meat had to be slaughtered according to Islamic law, with a swift cut and the name of God invoked, ensuring it was **halal** (permissible).

2. **Pork** was prohibited, so Muslims did not raise pigs. This shaped the livestock balance compared to Europe, where pork was common.

3. **Alcohol** was also forbidden in most interpretations of Islamic law, though some regions or individuals still consumed wine secretly. Officially, many cities replaced wine with drinks like fruit juices, **sherbet**, or water flavored with syrups (often from cherries, pomegranates, or rosewater).

These rules influenced trade as well. Regions under Islamic rule focused more on sheep, goat, or cattle, and found other ways to make up for not using pork. In some areas, Christians or Jews who lived under Muslim rule could raise pigs for their own use, but it remained a minority practice.

The Caliphs' Courts: Lavish Feasts and Cookbooks

Wealthy caliphs, sultans, or emirs hosted **extravagant banquets**. In cities like Baghdad or Samarra, the Abbasid court displayed its power by serving dozens of dishes, each heavily spiced or sweetened. Musicians, poets, and scholars provided entertainment, reflecting the empire's cultural achievements.

From these courts came some of the earliest written **cookbooks** in Arabic. Authors like **Ibn Sayyar al-Warraq** (10th century) or later writers compiled hundreds of recipes, giving us a glimpse of medieval Middle Eastern cuisine. These texts describe dishes such as rich meat stews with spices, layered pastries, and fruit syrups. They also offer advice on the health benefits of certain foods, drawing on Greek, Persian, and local medical traditions.

Presentation was key for royal banquets. Large platters might feature spiced lamb decorated with almonds and herbs, ringed by colorful fruit. Rice dishes could be molded into shapes or layered with saffron to create bright yellow color. Jars of scented rosewater or orange blossom water might be passed around for rinsing hands or adding fragrance to desserts.

Street Food and Markets

Not everyone dined in palaces. Everyday people in cities like **Cairo**, **Damascus**, or **Basra** bought **street food** from small vendors. These vendors sold grilled meats (kebabs), flatbreads, boiled beans, falafel-like fritters, sweet pastries soaked in honey, and refreshing sorbets made with snow from mountain peaks (in cooler regions).

Souks or **bazaars** were central to city life, with stalls overflowing with vegetables, fruits, spices, and textiles. Buyers haggled with merchants, taste-testing olives or dried figs. The variety of goods reflected the empire's wide-reaching trade, so city dwellers often ate more diverse diets than rural farmers.

Rural folks grew local crops—wheat, barley, dates in oasis areas—and kept goats or sheep. They might bake simple flatbreads on hot stones or in mud-brick ovens, making stews with whatever vegetables and legumes were available.

Influence of Persia and Other Cultures

The Abbasid Caliphate absorbed **Persian** cooking traditions, known for elegant rice dishes and use of fruits in savory meals (like apricots or pomegranates with lamb). **Persian literature**, like the epic poems of Ferdowsi, often described grand banquets. Even the concept of pairing sweet and sour in meat stews can trace roots to ancient Persian cuisine.

Turkic peoples from Central Asia also influenced Middle Eastern cooking as they migrated or conquered new lands. They brought techniques for grilling meats, making stuffed dumplings, and using dairy products like yogurt more extensively. Over time, these traditions blended with local ones to form the cuisines of places like Anatolia (modern Turkey).

In **Al-Andalus** (Muslim-ruled Spain), Islamic rulers oversaw advanced irrigation, introducing or expanding citrus groves, rice fields near Valencia, and sugarcane in the south. Local Spanish cooking merged with North African and Middle Eastern flavors, creating a unique blend that still echoes in the region's cuisine today.

The House of Wisdom and Food Knowledge

During the Islamic Golden Age, scholars gathered in places like **the House of Wisdom** in Baghdad to study and translate works from Greek, Indian, Persian, and other sources. This scholarly environment fostered interest in **medicine**, **astronomy**, **mathematics**, and of course, **agriculture** and **cooking**.

Writings from physicians like **Ibn Sina (Avicenna)** discussed the health effects of different foods, building on ancient knowledge of humors. They believed balanced diets could help maintain health. Cookbooks sometimes included medicinal advice: what spices were "hot" or "cold," which dishes aided digestion, or how certain herbs helped with illnesses.

This blend of scientific study, culinary experimentation, and cultural exchange created a refined dining culture among the educated and wealthy. However, common people still ate simpler meals, guided mostly by local traditions and availability of ingredients.

Sweets, Sorbets, and Innovative Beverages

With sugarcane plantations thriving, the Islamic Middle East became a hub for **sweet treats**. Popular desserts included:

- **Baklava-like pastries**: Layers of thin dough filled with nuts, sweetened with honey or sugar syrup.

- **Halva**: A dense sweet made from sesame paste or flour, sugar, and flavorings like rosewater or pistachios.

- **Candied fruits**: Apricots, plums, or citrus peels cooked in syrup, then dried.

Sorbets or sherbets were **fruit-flavored ices** sometimes made using snow carried from mountains (in areas that had them). These were luxurious, as cold storage was difficult. Cold beverages like **tamarind juice**, **rosewater sherbet**, or spiced fruit syrups offered relief in hot climates.

Coffee came into broader use later in this period or slightly after (it is believed coffee cultivation and the popular drink we know today spread from Ethiopia and Yemen over time). By the late medieval era, coffeehouses began to appear in some Middle Eastern cities, but they truly blossomed in the post-medieval Ottoman period, so their major impact on daily life came later.

Eating Customs and Manners

Muslim etiquette guided some aspects of dining. Many families ate **on low tables** or mats on the floor, using bread to scoop up food rather than utensils. Washing hands before and after meals was standard. At banquets, large communal platters might be shared among several people, each taking portions with the right hand.

In wealthier circles, there was also a sense of **refinement**—beautiful serving dishes, embroidered tablecloths, and decorative garnishes. Poetry and music might accompany the meal. Gifts of rare spices or sweets could be exchanged as tokens of respect.

Meanwhile, the **rural majority** followed simpler customs. A family might gather around a single pot of stew or soup, using spoons or bread to eat. Seasonal changes dictated their diet heavily; for instance, dates were harvested at certain times of year, providing both food and a trade product if surplus existed.

The Influence on Europe and Africa

Through trade, migration, and sometimes conflict (like the **Crusades**), aspects of Middle Eastern cuisine reached Europe. Crusaders returned with tastes for sugar, spices, and new fruits. Over centuries, some dishes or ingredients were adapted, especially in Mediterranean regions like Sicily or southern Italy, which were under Islamic rule for a while.

In North Africa, local Berber traditions mixed with Arab influences, creating dishes like **couscous** with spiced vegetables or meats. West African trade routes introduced items like kola nuts or unique spices into North African markets. The Islamic Golden Age acted as a bridge, spreading agricultural techniques, cookery ideas, and food-related knowledge far beyond the Middle East.

Legacy of the Medieval Middle East and the Islamic Golden Age

By the end of this era, the **Islamic world** had woven together diverse culinary customs—from Persian rice dishes to Levantine chickpea stews, Egyptian fava bean breakfasts, and Andalusian orange groves. Scholars preserved and expanded upon ancient agricultural knowledge, while traders carried spices, sugar, and fruits across three continents. Even though political power shifted—empires rose and fell—the deep-rooted food traditions continued, passing into the hands of later states and cultures.

Key contributions include:

1. **Advanced irrigation and farming** techniques that boosted crop variety.
2. The spread of **sugarcane** cultivation, leading to a sweet revolution in desserts.
3. The refinement of **spice blends**, marinade techniques, and sweet-sour flavor combinations.
4. The production of important **cookbooks**, preserving recipes and health advice that would influence future generations.

From the Middle East, we see how a mix of religion, commerce, and scholarship shaped both city and rural diets. In the **next chapters**, we will move on to other regions and times: the Mongol Empire and the Silk Road, the Pre-Columbian Americas, the Aztecs, Incas, and Mayas—each adding new pieces to our world tapestry of food history.

CHAPTER 13

The Mongol Empire and the Silk Road

When we think of the **Mongol Empire**, many people imagine galloping horsemen crossing vast grasslands. Indeed, for much of their history, Mongols were **nomadic herders** who roamed the Asian steppes. But their empire—founded by **Genghis Khan** in the early 13th century—grew to become one of the largest contiguous land empires in world history. It stretched from Eastern Europe across Central Asia all the way to parts of China and the Middle East.

This chapter looks at how the **food traditions** of these nomadic people blended with the **Silk Road** trade routes they controlled. We will see how the Mongol way of life affected what they ate, how they preserved their food, and how they influenced cuisine and trade across many regions.

The Mongol Homeland and Nomadic Life

The Mongols originally lived on the **steppes** of Central Asia—vast plains covered with grass. This land could be very harsh, with cold winters and dry summers. Farming was difficult, so the people **herded animals** like horses, sheep, goats, cattle, and yaks. They moved their herds across the grasslands in search of fresh pasture, living in **yurts** (round, portable tents also called **gers**).

Horses were central to Mongol life. They provided transportation, milk (mare's milk, known as **airag** or **kumis**), and even some meat. Other animals gave **milk**, **meat**, **wool**, and **skins**. Mongols relied heavily on **animal products** because plants were not abundant on the cold steppe. They did gather some wild herbs and roots in certain seasons, but these were less important than livestock.

Being **nomadic** meant the Mongols had to move camp many times a year. They needed food that could be easily carried and stored. This shaped their cooking methods—**drying**, **smoking**, and **fermenting** foods were essential to make them last during long journeys.

Staple Foods of the Mongols

1. **Dairy Products**: Mare's milk (airag or kumis) was a favorite drink. They also fermented milk from goats, sheep, or cows to make **yogurt**-like products. Cheeses and dried curds provided protein on the move.
2. **Meat**: Sheep, goats, and horses were the main sources. People roasted or boiled meat, cut it into strips to dry, or made it into stews when they set up camp.
3. **Borts (Dried Meat)**: Mongols often **air-dried** strips of meat—especially beef or mutton—to preserve it. Borts could last for months, and when needed, they could boil it in water to make a quick stew or soup.
4. **Grains (Later Adoption)**: Early Mongols had little access to grains, but as the empire expanded, they acquired wheat, millet, and rice from conquered regions. Nomadic families might trade livestock for flour or noodles, adding variety to their diets.

Despite this, the Mongols' diet remained **meat- and dairy-focused**. Vegetables and fruits were scarce on the steppe, so they became luxury items only when traded or taken from settled areas.

Genghis Khan's Conquests and Food Supplies

When **Genghis Khan** united the Mongol tribes around 1206, he led them on a campaign of expansion. His armies moved with incredible speed, thanks to their hardy horses and efficient tactics. They carried their **portable yurts** on carts, and each warrior had several horses. This let them switch mounts and travel farther each day.

But how did such armies eat on the march? The Mongols had to be self-sufficient:

- Warriors drank **horse's blood** in emergencies (a small cut to the horse's vein, not killing the animal) or mare's milk for energy.
- Dried meat (borts) or curd provided protein.
- They scouted farmland or took supplies from towns when entering more settled regions.

As the empire grew, Mongol leaders learned to **tax** the agricultural lands under their control, gaining a steady flow of **grain, produce, and tribute** from conquered peoples. This new wealth of ingredients began influencing Mongol cuisine, especially for the elite. Some Mongol nobles developed tastes for luxury goods—like **fruits, pastries, and spices**—they discovered in Persia or China.

Mongol Diet vs. Settled Societies

One key difference between Mongols and many of the people they conquered (like the Chinese, Persians, or Russians) was the **contrast** between a **nomadic, meat- and dairy-based diet** and the **agricultural, grain-based diets** of settled civilizations. In the Mongol Empire, these worlds collided:

- **Chinese cooking** prized vegetables, rice, and wheat-based noodles.
- **Persian cuisine** used fragrant spices, nuts, fruits in meat dishes, and elaborate rice preparations like pilaf.
- **Eastern European communities** relied on rye bread, cabbages, and root vegetables, along with some meats.

The Mongols might learn to enjoy **noodles** or **rice dishes**, especially in cities, while local populations sometimes adopted **fermented dairy** or dried meats. Over generations, the result was a **cultural exchange** that shaped food traditions across the empire.

The Silk Road: A Network of Exchange

Although the **Silk Road** trade routes between China and the Mediterranean existed long before the Mongols, the Mongol Empire's control made them safer and more unified than ever. Mongol leaders promoted **trade and communication**, protecting caravans with soldiers and establishing **relay stations** for messengers (the **yam** system).

This encouraged **merchants** from many lands to travel these routes. They carried valuable items:

- **Silk**, **porcelain**, and **tea** from China
- **Spices**, **herbs**, and **textiles** from India and Southeast Asia
- **Glassware**, **gold**, and **silver** from the Middle East
- **Furs**, **walrus ivory**, and **amber** from Russia or northern Europe

But these caravans also transported **food ideas** and **cooking techniques**. Spices and ingredients spread more widely, and recipes mingled in the great trading cities like **Karakorum**, **Samarkand**, **Bukhara**, and beyond.

Mongol Influence on Regional Cuisines

1. **China**: During the **Yuan Dynasty** (founded by Kublai Khan, Genghis's grandson), Mongol rulers embraced aspects of Chinese cuisine. Court banquets served both traditional Chinese dishes and Mongol favorites (like roasted mutton). Some historians think the Mongols helped spread **filled dumplings** or other wheat-based dishes to parts of China, though dumplings also have ancient local roots.
2. **Persia (Ilkhanate)**: Mongols in Persia adapted to local tastes, enjoying rice pilafs, kebabs, and sweet pastries. They introduced some fermented dairy habits, and the blending of Persian spices with Mongol meats likely created new stews and sauces.
3. **Central Asia**: Regions like Samarkand and Bukhara became vibrant crossroads of Persian, Turkish, Mongol, and Chinese influences. Plov (a type of pilaf), noodles, kebabs, dairy drinks, and stuffed pastries all merged in local cooking.
4. **Russia (Golden Horde)**: Mongol rule influenced Russian agriculture (e.g., an increase in horse breeding) and perhaps the introduction of certain fermenting techniques. However, the cold climate meant Russians still focused on rye bread, cabbages, and beets. Over time, Tatar and Mongol peoples in southern Russia developed new mixes of stewed meats, dumplings, and sour dairy dishes.

Each region took Mongol influences and wove them into its own traditions, sometimes making it hard to trace exact origins. But the era of Mongol unity clearly allowed for a more fluid exchange of **food knowledge**.

Cooking on the Move: Methods and Tools

Nomadic cooking had to be **simple**, using portable tools:

- **Metal cauldrons or large pots** for boiling water, soups, or stews. Hung over a central fire in a yurt or in the open air.

- **Spits** for roasting, though big roasts were more common in bigger camps.

- **Stones** to hold heat, which could be used to help cook certain dishes in ground pits.

- **Leather bags** or skins to hold liquids (milk, water) or for churning fermented dairy products.

They might toss dried meat into boiling water with salt or spices if they had them. Over time, as the empire connected them to new spices and grains, they might add onions, garlic, or millet to the pot. Spices from India or the Middle East, like cumin or coriander, gradually found their way into Mongol stews.

Fermentation was crucial. Mongols fermented milk into kumis, which could be slightly alcoholic and easier to digest than fresh mare's milk. They also developed dairy by-products like **aarul** (dried curd) that could be stored for long periods and reconstituted with water when needed.

Feasts and Hospitality in Mongol Culture

Even though they were nomadic, Mongols had a strong tradition of **hospitality**. A guest visiting a yurt would often be offered **tea** (later influenced by Chinese tea traditions) or a bowl of kumis and perhaps boiled mutton or dried meat. Wealthier camps or the Great Khan's palace might serve large roasted animals, assorted dairy products, and newly introduced delights (like sweet pastries from Middle Eastern recipes) for special events.

During major gatherings called **kurultai** (where leaders made decisions and celebrated alliances), food and drink flowed freely. Such events reinforced unity among Mongol nobles and showcased the empire's prosperity. Feasts sometimes included formal procedures for how to share mare's milk or portions of meat—reflecting respect for hierarchy and tradition.

City Life Under the Mongols: Karakorum and Beyond

As the Mongol Empire expanded, they established new capitals. **Karakorum** in Mongolia was one such city, though it was never huge by world standards. It served as a political and cultural center where ambassadors, merchants, and craftsmen from many lands gathered.

In Karakorum, you could find:

- **Markets** selling grain, spices, and handicrafts from as far as Persia or China.

- **Craftsmen** forging metal goods, building wagons, or weaving.

- **Palaces** where foreign advisors and Mongol chiefs dined on a mix of local meats and exotic goods.

Later, in China, **Kublai Khan** made **Beijing (Khanbaliq)** his capital when he formed the Yuan Dynasty. There, the Mongol court was exposed to Chinese banquets, with an array of dishes—steamed buns, noodles, vegetables, sweet desserts, and more. Mongol elites could indulge in fresh produce from southern China, while still cherishing their boiled mutton or kumis. This fusion at the Yuan court led to interesting crossovers in food traditions.

The Decline of the Mongol Empire and Its Food Legacy

By the late 14th century, the Mongol Empire fractured into smaller khanates. Local rulers in Persia, Russia, and China gradually took on their own identities, pushing out Mongol rule or mixing it with local traditions. However, the **Silk Road** routes and trading connections did not vanish. They continued to bring **spices, produce, and cooking ideas** across Asia and Europe, albeit under new leadership.

Timur (Tamerlane) and later Central Asian powers kept some steppe traditions alive, blending them with settled cultures. Mongol influences—like the respect for fermented dairy, the use of certain meats, or new cooking techniques—remained in local cuisines. Meanwhile, the memory of the Mongols as fierce warriors who also patronized trade and cultural exchange lingered throughout Eurasia.

Long-Term Impact on Culinary Exchange

Even after the empire faded, the **paths** and **connections** established under Mongol rule shaped global food history. For example:

- **Noodle dishes** or dumplings (like mantou or manti) traveled along the Silk Road. We see variations of stuffed dumplings in Central Asia, Russia (pelmeni), and East Asia—some may have gotten a boost from Mongol-era exchanges.
- The **use of fermented dairy** in parts of Central Asia, Russia, or the Middle East might have grown more common through nomadic influences.
- **Trade in spices, sugar, and other goods** continued with the knowledge that the Mongols had once made these routes safer. Future empires, like the Timurids or the Ming in China, built on that foundation.

In short, the Mongols did not invent all these foods or trade routes, but their empire bound them together in a unique way. This laid groundwork for future centuries of **culinary migration**.

CHAPTER 14

Food in Pre-Columbian Americas

Before Europeans set foot in the Americas, many diverse cultures and civilizations lived across these continents. We call this era **"Pre-Columbian,"** referring to the time before Christopher Columbus's first voyage in 1492. These peoples had their own methods of farming, hunting, gathering, and cooking, shaped by the varied landscapes—from Arctic tundra to tropical rainforests and high mountain ranges.

In this chapter, we explore the general food traditions of the Pre-Columbian Americas, focusing on how indigenous peoples cultivated unique crops like **maize (corn)**, **beans**, **squash**, and more. We will also see how they managed to feed large cities such as those built by the **Mayas**, the **Aztecs**, and other complex societies, setting the stage for significant cultural achievements long before European contact.

Geography and Diversity

The Americas span from the cold Arctic in the north to the temperate and tropical zones of Central and South America. With such a wide range of environments, Pre-Columbian peoples developed many different diets:

- **Arctic/Subarctic**: Native peoples relied on fishing, hunting sea mammals (seals, walruses), caribou, and gathering berries in short summers.

- **North American Plains**: Tribes chased huge herds of bison (buffalo) across grasslands. They used all parts of the animal for food, clothing, and tools.

- **Eastern Woodlands**: Farming communities grew maize, beans, and squash, alongside hunting deer and gathering nuts.

- **Southwestern Deserts**: Peoples like the Pueblo cultures relied on irrigated farming, growing corn, beans, squash, and cotton, along with desert-adapted wild foods.

- **Mesoamerica (Mexico and Central America)**: Complex civilizations like the Maya and Aztec cultivated maize, beans, squash, chili peppers, and more. They domesticated turkeys and developed advanced forms of agriculture.

- **Andean Region (South America)**: Civilizations such as the Inca built terraced farms for **potatoes**, **maize**, and **quinoa**. They raised llamas and alpacas for wool and meat.

Each region combined **farming** (where possible) with **hunting**, **fishing**, and **gathering**. Over centuries, they developed specialized crops that remain important around the world today.

Domestication of Crops

Corn (Maize) stands out as one of the greatest agricultural achievements in the Pre-Columbian world. Maize was bred from a wild grass called **teosinte** in Mesoamerica thousands of years ago. Through careful selection, indigenous farmers developed robust ears of corn. By the time of the Maya and Aztecs, maize was the central staple, processed in various ways—ground into flour for **tortillas**, boiled into hominy (posole), or eaten fresh.

Beans and Squash often grew alongside maize in a system called **"the Three Sisters."** Maize stalks provided a trellis for climbing bean vines, beans fixed nitrogen in the soil, and squash vines helped shade the ground, reducing weeds. This clever **companion planting** system spread through parts of North America and Mesoamerica.

Other Major Crops:

- **Potatoes**: Domesticated in the Andean highlands (modern-day Peru and Bolivia). The Incas cultivated hundreds of potato varieties suited to different altitudes. They also invented ways to preserve them, like **chuño** (freeze-dried potatoes).

- **Quinoa**: Another Andean crop, rich in protein. It thrived in harsh, high-altitude environments.

- **Tomatoes**, **chili peppers**, and **cacao** (for chocolate) were native to Mesoamerica. Chili peppers were especially widespread, adding spice to many dishes.

- **Peanuts**, **avocados**, **pineapples**, **papayas**, and **manioc** (cassava) all originated in the Americas, each linked to specific regions.

These plants represent an incredible agricultural heritage. Even now, they form the basis of many global cuisines, though in Pre-Columbian times they were tied to local customs and religious practices.

Hunting, Fishing, and Gathering

While agriculture was crucial in many areas, hunting and fishing remained vital for protein. Different regions specialized in certain animals:

- **Plains** tribes like the **Lakota** or **Comanche** hunted bison in big communal hunts. They made **pemmican** by mixing dried bison meat with fat and berries—a high-energy food that could last months.

- **Eastern Woodlands** peoples hunted deer, turkey, rabbit, and trapped smaller game.

- **Coastal** communities fished for salmon, cod, shellfish, and seals. In the Pacific Northwest, tribes constructed elaborate wooden fish traps to catch migrating salmon.

- **Rainforest** dwellers in the Amazon region hunted monkeys, birds, and tapirs, while also gathering fruits, nuts (like Brazil nuts), and tubers.

Gathering wild foods—berries, nuts, roots, and edible greens—supplemented diets everywhere. For instance, in the Great Lakes region, peoples harvested **wild rice** (a native aquatic grass) from lakes and marshes.

Cooking Methods and Tools

Pre-Columbian peoples used **simple but effective** cooking tools:

- **Earthen or clay pots**: For boiling soups, stews, or preparing maize dough.

- **Stone griddles** or **flat stones**: For baking flatbreads like tortillas.

- **Pit ovens**: Hot rocks in a pit would slow-cook meats or root vegetables underground.

- **Wooden or bone utensils**: Spoons, ladles, or stirring sticks. Metal was rare in most of the Americas before European contact, though Andean cultures worked with gold, silver, and copper for ornaments and tools.

Nixtamalization is a special process used primarily in Mesoamerica: maize kernels are soaked in an alkaline solution (water with ashes or lime) to remove the hull. This **increases the nutritional value** of corn, making vitamins more accessible and improving dough quality for tortillas or tamales. This was a critical discovery in Mesoamerican cooking.

Seasonings varied by region. Chili peppers, wild herbs, and salt (extracted from salt ponds or traded) were common in some places. In the Andes, local herbs like huacatay might flavor stews. In the Amazon, indigenous communities might use peppers or wild aromatic leaves.

Maya, Aztec, and Other Mesoamerican Cultures

Maya civilization thrived in the rainforests and highlands of Central America. They built cities with temples, pyramids, and a well-developed writing system. Maize was central to their diet and religion—many Maya myths describe humans as being made from corn dough. They also ate beans, squash, chili peppers, tropical fruits, and turkey or dog in some areas. Fishing and gathering shellfish were important along the coasts.

Aztecs (in the region of modern central Mexico) were known for their large capital, **Tenochtitlan**, built on Lake Texcoco. They used **chinampas**—floating garden beds—to grow maize, beans, squash, tomatoes, and more. Chili peppers, amaranth, and **cacao** (used to make a chocolate drink) were also prized. Aztecs domesticated **turkeys** and kept **dogs** (xoloitzcuintli) for meat, though dog consumption varied by region. They fished in the lake and gathered water plants like **spirulina** (tecuítlatl) as a protein source.

Religious ceremonies often involved **food offerings** to gods, especially maize and chocolate. Elite Aztecs might enjoy spiced cocoa drinks sweetened with honey or flavored with vanilla pods (a native orchid). Markets in Tenochtitlan sold produce from all over the empire, showcasing a wide variety of local foods.

The Andes: Inca Empire and Highland Farming

In South America, the **Inca Empire** grew along the Andes Mountains, with the capital at **Cusco**. Their advanced **terrace farming** turned steep slopes into productive fields. They grew **potatoes**, **maize**, **quinoa**, **peanuts**, and **peppers**. Llamas and alpacas provided meat, wool, and transportation. **Guinea pigs** (cuy) were also raised for meat in some Andean communities.

Freeze-Drying: High altitude and cold nights allowed the Incas to freeze-dry potatoes into **chuño**—which lasted for months or years. Maize could be toasted or turned into **chicha** (fermented corn drink). The empire's extensive road system connected farmland to cities, enabling surplus produce to be stored in state warehouses (qollqas). In times of famine, the government could distribute stored foods, helping the empire remain stable.

Other Remarkable Pre-Columbian Cultures

1. **Ancestral Puebloans (Southwestern USA)**: Built cliff dwellings (like those at Mesa Verde) and large pueblos. They farmed maize, beans, and squash using irrigation techniques. They also gathered wild plants like piñon nuts.

2. **Mississippian Cultures (Eastern USA)**: Constructed large earthen mounds for ceremonial sites. They cultivated the Three Sisters (maize, beans, squash), along with sunflowers and other local plants. The city of **Cahokia** was a major center around the 10th–14th centuries.

3. **Taino (Caribbean)**: Grew **cassava (yuca)**, sweet potatoes, beans, and peppers. Cassava bread was a staple. They also fished and collected shellfish.

4. **Amazon Basin Cultures**: Practiced slash-and-burn agriculture to plant manioc, maize, and fruits, while also hunting and fishing the abundant rainforest and river species. They used canoes to navigate the vast river system.

Each culture had unique traditions, but they shared innovations like **domesticating local plants**, managing land effectively, and balancing farming with hunting or gathering to survive in different ecosystems.

Food and Religious Beliefs

Many Pre-Columbian peoples saw **food** as a **sacred gift** from the gods. In Mesoamerica, for instance, **maize** was central to cosmology. The Maya and Aztecs held festivals honoring the maize deity, offering the first harvest or special dishes to ensure future fertility.

The **Incas** sacrificed llamas or even offered precious foods to mountain deities (apus) and the Sun god (Inti). Important rituals involved **chicha**, the corn beer that had ceremonial significance. Feasts during festivals were a way to unite communities, celebrate good harvests, and honor ancestors.

In everyday life, families might pray or perform small rituals before planting or hunting. This spiritual connection underscored the importance of maintaining balance with nature—taking only what was needed and showing gratitude for the land's bounty.

Trade Networks and Food Exchange

Long before Europeans arrived, indigenous peoples created **trade networks** that spanned great distances:

- **Mesoamerican** traders moved cacao beans, obsidian, salt, and exotic feathers across various city-states.

- **South American** routes carried chili peppers, peanuts, textiles, and precious metals along the Andes.

- **North American** groups bartered maize for furs or traded coastal shells for inland goods.

These exchanges spread certain crops beyond their original homelands. For instance, maize reached parts of North America, where it became essential to the diets of many tribes. Similarly, **cacao** might travel from the Maya region to other areas for ritual use.

Storage and Preservation

To handle seasonal changes or crop failures, indigenous peoples used **storage techniques**:

- **Drying** or **smoking** meat, fish, and surplus produce.

- **Underground pits** to store tubers or root vegetables in cooler conditions.

- **Pottery containers** or baskets sealed with resins to keep grain safe from moisture and pests.

- **Incas** used freeze-drying (chuño) for potatoes and stored them in warehouses for distribution.

These methods helped maintain a steady food supply, ensuring large populations could thrive in cities like Tenochtitlan or Cusco.

Everyday Meals vs. Feasts

An **ordinary** meal for a Maya farmer might be **maize tortillas** with a bean paste, chili sauce, and maybe some wild greens. An Aztec merchant in Tenochtitlan could enjoy **tamales** stuffed with beans or turkey, topped with a chili sauce. Meanwhile, a small Andean village family might eat **potato stew** with peppers, occasionally flavoring it with alpaca or guinea pig.

For **major ceremonies**, communities came together in feasts that could feature abundant servings of staple foods—maize-based dishes, roasted meat, fish, local fruits, or special drinks like **chicha** or **cacao**. Musicians, dancers, and religious leaders performed rites, linking food with cosmic and social harmony.

Regional Specialties and Culinary Creativity

Chili Peppers: Mesoamericans had many varieties—mild to very hot—and used them fresh or dried. They formed the base of countless sauces (moles) combined with seeds, nuts, or herbs.

Chocolate: Made from **cacao beans** fermented, roasted, ground into a paste, and mixed with water. Sometimes spiced with chili or flavored with honey or vanilla. Originally a bitter beverage, it was often consumed by nobles or used in rituals.

Tamales: Maize dough (masa) wrapped in corn husks or banana leaves, steamed with fillings. Varieties ranged from plain to complex (with meats, beans, or vegetables).

Inca Stews: Combined potatoes, maize kernels (choclo), hot peppers (ajís), and sometimes dried llama meat. The sauce could be thickened or flavored with local herbs.

Ceviche-like dishes in some coastal areas: Raw or lightly cooked fish marinated in juices or peppers, though modern ceviche is more associated with post-Columbian influences. Still, the idea of marinating fish with acidic fruit or spices may have local precedents.

Pre-Columbian Food Legacy

Despite the devastation that came with European colonization later, many **Pre-Columbian crops and cooking methods** survived and spread worldwide. Today, foods like **corn, tomatoes, potatoes, chili peppers, and cocoa** are staples in global cuisines—from Italian pasta sauce (tomatoes) to Indian curries (chili peppers) to Irish stew (potatoes). The original knowledge of farming, companion planting, and creative cooking was developed by countless generations of indigenous Americans.

In their own time, these societies formed robust food systems—**irrigation** in deserts, **terracing** in mountains, **chinampas** on lakes, **pemmican** on plains, and much more. They balanced local resources with social and religious practices that respected the environment's gifts. Whether it was the Maya in lush rainforests or the Inca in rugged Andes, their success shows human adaptability and innovation long before outside influences arrived.

CHAPTER 15

Aztecs, Incas, and Mayas

In our previous chapter about the Pre-Columbian Americas, we saw how many different indigenous peoples had their own ways of farming, hunting, and cooking. Now, in Chapter 15, we will take a **closer look** at three major civilizations in the Americas: the **Aztecs**, the **Incas**, and the **Mayas**. These societies each developed unique cultures, built impressive cities, and managed advanced food systems that supported large populations. We will explore what they grew, how they cooked, and how food was woven into their religions, governments, and social life.

The Aztecs: Masters of the Valley of Mexico

The **Aztecs** lived in the area that is now central Mexico, especially around the large lake system in the Valley of Mexico. Their powerful city, **Tenochtitlan**, was founded on an island in the middle of **Lake Texcoco** and eventually became one of the biggest cities in the Pre-Columbian Americas. The Aztecs rose to prominence in the 14th century, forming alliances with neighboring city-states. Over time, they built an empire that demanded tribute in the form of goods—often including food—from conquered regions.

Aztec Agriculture: Chinampas and More

One of the Aztecs' most striking farming methods was the use of **chinampas**, sometimes called "floating gardens." These were man-made plots built up in the shallow parts of lakes. Farmers drove wooden stakes into the lakebed, wove reeds between them, and filled the area with mud, algae, and decaying plant matter. Over time, these chinampas became fertile patches of land where the Aztecs grew maize, beans, squash, tomatoes, chili peppers, amaranth, and flowers.

- **Maize**: The main staple, turned into tortillas, tamales, and a variety of porridges.

- **Beans**: High in protein, often boiled or mashed, then seasoned with chili or other flavorings.
- **Squash and Chili Peppers**: Provided vitamins and flavor. Squash seeds were also eaten for protein and healthy fats.
- **Amaranth**: A grain-like crop used in porridge and sometimes made into ceremonial dough figurines mixed with honey.

Chinampas were incredibly productive. They were surrounded by water channels, which made irrigation easier. The soil was rich in nutrients because farmers could scoop mud from the lakebed to refresh the plots. This system fed thousands of people and helped Tenochtitlan grow into a bustling urban center.

Markets, Tribute, and Food Abundance

Tenochtitlan had grand marketplaces—especially the one in **Tlatelolco**—where people could buy and sell food items, pottery, textiles, and more. Farmers from all around the region brought produce to trade, while merchants carried in goods like **cacao beans**, tropical fruits, or dried fish from distant provinces.

The Aztec empire also demanded **tribute** from conquered peoples. These subject city-states often paid in food products—like maize, beans, chilies, or cotton. As a result, Tenochtitlan enjoyed a steady stream of supplies, which the rulers used to feed nobles, warriors, and priests.

Everyday Meals and Special Dishes

A typical Aztec meal might include:

- **Tortillas** made from nixtamalized maize dough (masa).

- A **bean mash** or stew.

- A sauce or relish made with **chili peppers** and herbs.

- Vegetables like tomatoes or squash, often boiled or grilled.

- Occasional additions of turkey or other meat (for those who could afford it).

For the elite, meats such as **turkey**, **duck**, or even hairless dogs (xoloitzcuintli) could appear at feasts. They also enjoyed fish brought from coastal areas. Priests and nobles sometimes drank a **cacao-based beverage**—spiced with chili, vanilla, or honey—seen as a luxury drink.

Religious ceremonies might include special tamales shaped or decorated for the gods, or large banquets where entire communities participated. Many Aztec deities were connected to agriculture, especially maize gods, and offerings of food were a key part of keeping the cosmic balance.

The Incas: Masters of the Andes

While the Aztecs ruled in Mexico, the **Inca Empire** dominated the Andean region of South America. Their capital city was **Cusco**, high in the mountains. The Incas built a network of roads across rugged terrain, uniting diverse climates and cultures under one imperial system. Their ability to farm steep slopes, store surplus produce, and distribute food in times of need was a key to their success.

Terraced Farming and Crop Diversity

In the Andes, flat land was scarce, so the Incas created **terraces** along mountain slopes. They built stone retaining walls and filled them with fertile soil. These terraces helped conserve water, reduce erosion, and enable farming at high altitudes. Crops included:

1. **Potatoes**: Hundreds of varieties, adapted to different altitudes.

2. **Maize**: Grown in lower, warmer valleys.

3. **Quinoa**: Rich in protein, hardy enough for cooler highlands.

4. **Peanuts**, **chili peppers**, **beans**, **tomatoes**, and **fruit** in suitable microclimates.

Llamas and alpacas provided meat, wool, and transport. **Guinea pigs** (cuy) were also raised as a source of protein, especially in household settings. Where the climate was too cold for many vegetables, the Incas still had potatoes and hardy grains.

Storehouses and Food Security

A hallmark of Inca administration was the **state-owned storehouses** (qollqas). Local officials collected portions of each harvest, storing potatoes, maize, dried meat (ch'arki), and other goods. Thanks to the cold, dry mountain air and preservation techniques like **freeze-drying** potatoes into **chuño**, these supplies lasted a long time.

When a region suffered a poor harvest or faced natural disasters, the Inca bureaucracy could **distribute stored food** to prevent famine. This strategy supported large construction projects—like roads, bridges, and temples—because workers knew they would be fed.

Meals and Cooking in the Andes

The Incas boiled or roasted potatoes, or turned them into **chuño** by leaving them out in the cold nights and sunny days to freeze-dry. They prepared **stews** of llama or alpaca meat with vegetables and chili peppers (ajís). **Chicha**, a fermented corn drink, was central in religious ceremonies and social gatherings. People also consumed a range of sauces made with local herbs or peppers, served over quinoa or tubers.

For everyday families in a village, meals often centered on **potatoes**—fresh or dried—mixed with peppers and maybe small amounts of meat. In special feasts, they might roast a llama or share large amounts of chicha. Festivals honoring the sun god (Inti) or local mountain spirits featured communal meals, singing, and dancing.

The Mayas: Masters of Mesoamerican Rainforests and Highlands

While the Aztecs rose in Central Mexico and the Incas in the Andes, the **Maya** civilization flourished in the rainforests and highlands of southeastern Mexico, Guatemala, Belize, and parts of Honduras and El Salvador. The Maya had reached impressive cultural heights centuries before the Aztecs, though city-states continued to exist into the Postclassic period. Known for their **hieroglyphic writing**, astronomical knowledge, and grand temple-pyramids, the Maya also developed advanced agriculture systems suited to rainforest environments.

Slash-and-Burn and Milpas

In many Maya regions, soils were thin and easily exhausted, so farmers often used **slash-and-burn** (also called milpa) methods. They cleared a patch of forest, burned the debris to return nutrients to the soil, then planted a diverse array of crops. Like other Mesoamerican cultures, the **Three Sisters**—maize, beans, and squash—were key. Over time, the field might be left fallow to let the forest recover, and new patches would be cleared elsewhere.

In the **Maya highlands**, terraces and irrigation canals sometimes replaced slash-and-burn, ensuring a more permanent agriculture. Maya farmers grew many of the same crops we see among the Aztecs: maize, beans, chilies, and squash, as well as fruits like papaya and avocado. They also cultivated **cacao** as both a food item and a form of currency.

Elaborate Cuisine and Rituals

Maize had deep religious significance among the Maya. Their myths describe humans as created from **maize dough** by the gods. Ritual offerings of tamales and other maize foods were crucial in ceremonies. **Cacao** was also revered—Maya nobility enjoyed chocolate drinks often flavored with chili, annatto (to add reddish color), and wild honey.

Mayas might cook:

- **Stews** with chili peppers, tomatoes, and local herbs.
- **Tamales** wrapped in banana leaves (especially in the southern areas) or corn husks (more common in the north).
- Various dips and sauces made from ground seeds, chili peppers, and sometimes pumpkin seeds (a type of early mole).

As in many Mesoamerican cultures, **turkeys** and dogs were domesticated for meat, and wild game like deer or peccary supplemented protein. Fishing and gathering shellfish were common in coastal areas. Daily meals likely included thick maize-based porridges or tortillas, spiced with chili or eaten alongside beans.

Trade and City-States

Maya city-states traded regionally, moving salt, cacao, feathers, obsidian, and jade between lowland and highland areas. Farmers brought produce to markets near large city centers, exchanging it for pottery, tools, or woven goods. Though Maya cities rose and fell at different times, their agriculture and food traditions persisted, adapted to local environments and power structures.

Comparisons and Shared Legacies

Aztecs, Incas, and Mayas each used different farming methods, shaped by their landscapes. The Aztecs mastered chinampas in shallow lakes, the Incas built terraced farms in the high Andes, and the Maya managed rainforests with slash-and-burn or terraces in the highlands. Yet they all relied on staple crops—**maize** being the cornerstone in Mesoamerica, with the Andes focusing heavily on **potatoes** and other tubers as well. Beans, chili peppers, squash, and specialized local plants also played important roles.

All three valued **communal feasting** and religious rites featuring food. Nobles or priests often had more elaborate dishes, sweetened with honey or combined with spices, while commoners stuck to simpler stews, tortillas, or potato-based meals. Nonetheless, these societies developed ways to store surplus produce (Inca storehouses, Aztec tribute systems) and to handle environmental challenges (like mountainous terrain or dense forests).

Though each eventually fell under Spanish conquest, the **food traditions** they nurtured continue in modern times in various local forms—tortillas, tamales, potato dishes, chili sauces, and more. These Pre-Columbian civilizations left an enormous impact on global diets once their crops (maize, potatoes, tomatoes, etc.) spread to other continents.

CHAPTER 16

Viking Age and Northern Europe

The **Viking Age** (roughly late 8th to mid-11th century) was a time when seafaring Norse people from Scandinavia—modern-day Norway, Sweden, and Denmark—raided, traded, and settled across wide areas of Europe and beyond. They reached parts of Britain, Ireland, France, Russia, Iceland, Greenland, and even briefly North America. Though famous for raids, Vikings were also **skilled traders** and **farmers** who brought their own culinary traditions wherever they traveled.

In this chapter, we will explore Viking food customs and, more broadly, **Northern European** food life during the early medieval period. We will learn about farming in colder climates, the importance of fish and dairy, and how the Vikings used trade routes to gather exotic ingredients from faraway lands.

The Northern Climate and Farming Challenges

Scandinavia's landscape includes **fjords**, **mountains**, **forests**, and **coastal plains**. Winters are long and cold, summers short and often mild. Farming is possible, but the growing season is short. As a result, Norse people focused on **hardy crops** and **animal husbandry**:

- **Barley, rye, and oats**: These grains could handle cooler, wetter conditions better than wheat.

- **Vegetables**: Cabbages, onions, and root vegetables like turnips or carrots (usually older varieties, not the bright orange modern type).

- **Livestock**: Cattle, sheep, goats, pigs, and chickens. Cattle provided milk for butter and cheese, while sheep gave wool for clothing. Pigs were fed on forest acorns in some areas.

- **Horses**: Used mainly for transport, though smaller in size than modern breeds.

Because farmland was limited, **fishing** and **hunting** were also important. Coastal communities caught cod, herring, salmon, and other fish. Inland, people hunted deer or elk in forests, though agriculture slowly replaced large-scale hunting as the main food source.

Viking Households and Food Preservation

Most Vikings lived on **small farms** or in villages. A typical farm had a **longhouse**—a rectangular building with a central hearth for cooking and warmth. Family, hired workers, and sometimes animals shared this space in the cold months. Food was stored in **sheds** or outbuildings, kept as cool and dry as possible.

Preservation was crucial:

1. **Smoking** fish or meat in a small shed.

2. **Salting** cod or herring.

3. **Drying** fish on racks near the coast.

4. **Fermenting** or pickling in brine.

5. **Turning milk** into butter, cheese, or sour dairy products.

During winter, fresh vegetables were rare. People relied on **stored root vegetables** or dried legumes. Meats salted in barrels and dried fish could last through the cold months. Dairy cows provided milk in warmer seasons, but production dropped in winter, so **cheese** or **butter** were ways to save the summer surplus.

Everyday Viking Meals

A typical Viking meal might include:

- A **thick porridge** or bread made from barley or rye.

- A **stew** containing salted or smoked meat, onions, and root vegetables.

- **Fish** (fresh, dried, or salted) boiled or roasted.

- **Ale** or **mead** (fermented honey drink) to drink, if available. Otherwise, water from wells or streams.

Breakfast (sometimes just leftover stew or bread) got people started. The main meal in the early evening included heartier portions, especially after fieldwork or fishing. Vikings likely ate with **wooden bowls, trenchers of bread**, or sometimes simple pottery. Spoons and knives were common; forks were less typical in this period.

Herbs such as dill, thyme, or wild onions might flavor soups. Sea salt or local salt sources were limited and valuable. Honey sweetened rare treats but was not plentiful in all areas. Vikings also used **wild berries**—lingonberries, cloudberries, bilberries—for fresh eating or preserves.

Feasts and Gatherings

Vikings enjoyed **feasting** for important events—harvest festivals, weddings, religious ceremonies, or to honor guests. Wealthy chieftains or jarls hosted large gatherings in the **longhouse**. They served roasted meats—like pork, mutton, or beef—alongside bread, butter, and ale or mead. Drinking horns or wooden cups passed among guests. **Skalds** (poets) might recite epic tales, and musicians played simple string or wind instruments.

Large feasts also required **plenty of supplies**. Chieftains who wanted to display generosity needed big herds, successful hunts, or well-managed fishing. In winter, festive meals might include salted fish or smoked meats, rehydrated and cooked into tasty stews. Berries stored in honey or mead could become a sweet sauce or dessert.

Viking Raids and Trade: Food on the Move

When Vikings set out on longships for raids or exploration, they carried **preserved food**—barrels of salted fish or meat, sacks of dried bread or grain, and possibly cheese. They also fished or foraged along the way. If raids succeeded, they might seize livestock or grain stores from coastal settlements. This was harsh for those being raided but gave Vikings fresh supplies.

However, Vikings were not just raiders—they were also **traders**. Norse merchants traveled down rivers in Eastern Europe, reaching markets in Byzantium (Constantinople) and the Arab world. They brought **furs, walrus ivory, and slaves**, and returned with **silver, spices, wine, and possibly dried fruits**. Over time, some wealthier Viking households gained access to **exotic items** like raisins or fine wheaten bread from southern lands. Yet these luxuries were beyond the reach of ordinary farmers.

Norse Beliefs and Food

Norse mythology featured gods like Odin, Thor, and Freya. Feasting in **Valhalla**—the hall of the slain—was a famous image of the afterlife for warriors, where they would enjoy endless meat and mead. Certain ceremonies might involve animal sacrifices (like a pig or horse) to gain the favor of gods, with the meat then shared among participants in a feast.

Seasonal festivals, such as the midwinter **Yule**, involved feasting and possibly the offering of a boar (the "Sonargöltr") to ensure fertility for crops and livestock. Over time, as Christianity spread in Scandinavia, older pagan customs blended with new Christian feasts, maintaining a cycle of communal meals in village life.

Connections Across Northern Europe

Though the Vikings dominated the seas, other peoples in Northern Europe shared similar food challenges and solutions:

- **Anglo-Saxons** in England: Grew wheat in warmer southern areas, barley and rye elsewhere, raised pigs in forested regions, and used fish from rivers and coasts.

- **Frisians** and other coastal Germans: Relied on cattle, dairy, and dikes to reclaim land from the sea.

- **Celts** in Scotland, Ireland, and Wales: Grew oats, barley, and raised cattle or sheep. The climate also supported root vegetables and hardy greens.

Trade and migration meant these groups influenced each other. Norse settlers in **Normandy** (France) introduced certain fishing or dairy methods, while picking up local bread-baking skills. In the **Danelaw** region of England, Norse farmers integrated with Anglo-Saxons, sharing grain varieties and cooking ideas.

Evolution of Food During the Viking Age

From the late 8th century onward, more land was cleared in Scandinavia for farms, especially in Denmark's milder climate. Towns like **Hedeby** or **Birka** grew into trade hubs. Archaeological digs reveal **grindstones** for flour, pottery for cooking, remains of salted herring or cod, and occasionally imported goods like walnuts or exotic spices. By the end of the Viking Age (around the 11th century), stronger kingdoms formed (Denmark, Norway, Sweden), and Christianity spread widely.

This period saw:

1. **Better iron tools** (scythes, plows) for improved farming.
2. **Greater trade** networks bringing new ingredients (even small amounts of wine or dried fruits).
3. **Conversion to Christianity**, reshaping feast days and religious dietary rules.
4. **Integration** of Norse diets with local ones in places they settled, like northern England, the Scottish Isles, or parts of Ireland.

Typical Dishes and Flavors

Bread was often coarse, made from barley or rye flour, sometimes flat or dense loaves. **Porridges** or gruels could include grains boiled in water or milk. **Stews** were common, with meat, onions, and root vegetables simmered together. Fish could be boiled in a pot with herbs and served with bread or leftover grains.

Mead, made from fermented honey, was the signature festive drink. **Ale** was brewed from barley, though it might be weaker than many modern beers. Spices like pepper or cumin were expensive imports, so local seasonings included wild herbs, salt, or onion-type plants. Sweet treats were rare—perhaps dried apples, berries, or bread sweetened with honey if available.

Seafarers in the Viking Age had to be practical, but they also knew how to enjoy a good feast when circumstances allowed. Feasts bonded communities, rewarded loyal warriors, and honored gods or Christian saints (in later times).

Trade Routes: Linking North and South

The **Varangian** routes down Russian rivers brought Vikings to the Black Sea and Caspian Sea, connecting them with Byzantine and Islamic markets. North-South trade meant that certain goods—like **walnuts, dried grapes (raisins), or saffron**—occasionally found their way to Scandinavian towns. While these items remained high-status luxuries, they influenced the palates of wealthier Norse families.

On the western side, Vikings traveled to **Iceland**, **Greenland**, and even glimpsed **Vinland** (Newfoundland) in North America. Iceland's volcanic soils allowed for some barley and hay but not much else, so Icelanders relied heavily on **sheep, cattle**, and **fishing**. Greenland settlements focused on **seals, caribou**, and maritime resources. These expansions highlight the Vikings' adaptability: they used local resources, stored food for winter, and imported what they could from Europe.

The Influence of Viking Food Traditions

As the Viking Age ended and medieval kingdoms took form in Northern Europe, many Norse culinary customs blended with local traditions:

1. **Preservation techniques** (drying, salting, smoking) remained crucial in regions with short growing seasons.

2. **Dairy** products—cheese, butter, sour milk—continued to be staples.

3. **Bread** from barley, rye, and sometimes wheat (in warmer areas) stayed central.

4. **Fish** consumption remained high, especially salted herring and cod, forming the basis of trade in later centuries (e.g., the Hanseatic League).

Though the Vikings are often remembered for raids, they were also farmers, fishers, and traders with a resourceful food culture shaped by the demands of their environment. Their legacy includes a shared Northern European love of robust breads, preserved fish, hearty stews, and communal feasting traditions.

CHAPTER 17

Renaissance Food in Europe

The word "Renaissance" means "rebirth." This period—often placed between the 14th and 17th centuries in Europe—followed the Middle Ages. It saw major changes in **art**, **science**, and **philosophy**, as people rediscovered ancient Greek and Roman ideas and combined them with new thinking. Cities like **Florence**, **Venice**, and **Rome** in Italy became centers of creativity. Wealthy merchants and noble families sponsored artists, architects, and scholars. Alongside these cultural changes, people's eating habits and ideas about food also began to shift.

During the Renaissance, Europe recovered from the worst of medieval famines, plagues, and warfare. **Trade routes** expanded, money-based economies grew, and wealthy families competed to show off their power with fine clothing, art, and—of course—lavish feasts. As a result, new ingredients, cooking methods, and dining customs spread across the continent, especially among the upper classes.

The Shift from Medieval to Renaissance Food Culture

In many ways, **Renaissance cuisine** continued medieval traditions, with bread, pottages, meats, and local vegetables forming the base of daily diets. Most common people still ate coarser bread, limited meat, and simple stews. However, among the wealthy elites—nobles, merchants, and royal courts—several changes became noticeable:

1. **New Ingredients**: Thanks to better trade, more people could get **sugar**, **rice**, dried fruits (like raisins or prunes), and spices.

2. **Greater Emphasis on Presentation**: Banquets became a showcase, with elaborate table decorations and carefully arranged dishes.

3. **Influence of Ancient Texts**: Scholars read Greek and Roman works on diet, health, and banqueting (like those by Galen or Apicius), inspiring new ways to think about balanced meals or flavor combinations.

4. **Regional Specialties**: As cities became richer, local areas developed signature dishes, often influenced by foreign ideas introduced through merchants.

Still, the majority of Europeans lived as peasants in rural areas, focusing on farming to produce enough for their families or feudal lords. The grand banquets and the changes in cooking styles mainly affected the upper echelons of society.

Italy: Center of Renaissance Cuisine

Though the Renaissance spread across Europe, **Italy** often stands out as a major starting point. Wealthy city-states like **Florence**, **Milan**, and **Venice** had thriving trade networks, bringing in goods from the Mediterranean and beyond. Rich families—like the **Medici** in Florence—patronized art and scholarship, and their courts became places where new dishes were invented or refined.

Italian cooks became known for their skillful use of:

- **Olive oil** and fresh herbs (basil, rosemary, sage).

- **Cheeses** (Parmesan was already famous in some regions).

- **Pasta**: By the Renaissance, dried pasta was increasingly common in parts of Italy, though fresh pastas (like ravioli or lasagna) also appeared in wealthy households.

- **Rice** dishes, especially in northern Italy, where risotto started to develop (with saffron or other flavorings).

- **Sweets** flavored with sugar, almond paste (marzipan), or citrus peels.

As the Renaissance advanced, some Italian cookbooks appeared, showcasing recipes that balanced sweet and savory flavors. The concept of **sauce-making** also became more refined, with cooks using herbs, spices, or meat stocks to create layered tastes.

France and Its Growing Food Reputation

Across the Alps, **France** also emerged as a center of sophisticated dining. The French court, especially in the 16th and 17th centuries, became a major influencer of European taste. Well before the famous "Haute Cuisine" of later eras, Renaissance France saw the seeds of elegant dining. Royals like **Francis I** (early 16th century) and later **Henry IV** championed lavish feasts with multiple courses.

Medieval French dishes like heavily spiced roasts or thick sauces began to change. By the late Renaissance, simpler flavor combinations emerged, focusing on fewer spices but higher-quality ingredients like fresh butter, cream, wine, and herbs (parsley, chervil, tarragon). However, these developments were still mostly limited to noble households and did not represent the diets of ordinary villagers, who relied on dark bread, onions, root vegetables, and occasional meat or fish.

Renaissance Banquets: Extravagance and Show

Noble families and royal courts used **banquets** to display wealth and status. These meals featured multiple courses—perhaps as many as six or more. Each course might include several dishes. Guests sat at long tables, sometimes separated by rank. Servants brought in large trays of food.

Presentation was key. Foods could be colored with natural dyes—like saffron for yellow, spinach or parsley for green, and cochineal (an insect dye) for red. Pastry chefs molded sugar or marzipan into shapes of animals, castles, or mythical scenes. Peacocks might be roasted, then dressed again in their feathers to amaze diners. While some of these "entremets" (show dishes) continued from medieval times, Renaissance banquets often became even more elaborate, with music and theatrical performances woven into the meal.

Table Manners also evolved. Forks (in some Italian courts) began to appear more frequently, though many still ate with knives, spoons, or their fingers, using bread as a trencher. Washing hands before a meal became more common, and elaborate table linens reflected new ideas about cleanliness and style.

The Impact of Commerce and Exploration

During the Renaissance, European **exploration** accelerated, especially after the Portuguese reached new sea routes to Africa and Asia. The Italian city-states had long been middlemen in spice trade, bringing **pepper, cinnamon, cloves, nutmeg**, and other exotic goods from the Middle East. Now, Portuguese and Spanish ships sailed around Africa or across the Atlantic, seeking direct access to spice-producing regions.

In the early Renaissance, the main spice trade still went through the eastern Mediterranean, controlled by Venice, Genoa, and other powers. This made spices still quite expensive, so only the well-off used them freely. Even so, the thirst for spices was a major driver of commerce, and Renaissance merchants grew rich from these trades, reinforcing the cultural emphasis on elaborate, spice-infused feasts. We will discuss this more in Chapter 18 on the Spice Routes.

Influence of Humanism and Ancient Texts on Diet

Humanism was a key intellectual movement of the Renaissance. Scholars looked to ancient Greece and Rome for inspiration, copying old manuscripts on various subjects, including **medical** and **dietary** advice. They rediscovered texts by **Galen**, who had written about the four humors (blood, phlegm, yellow bile, black bile) and how different foods could balance these humors in the body. Renaissance doctors and cooks combined these ideas with their own experiences.

While not everyone believed the same theories, many wealthy households hired physicians to advise on diets. Foods were sometimes classified as "hot" or "cold," "moist" or "dry," and the perfect meal balanced these qualities. Richer folks tried to show they were sophisticated by following such advice, even if the underlying science was not what we would use today.

Common People's Food vs. Nobles' Feasts

We should not forget that most Europeans were still **peasants** or **town laborers**. Their daily meals changed more slowly and involved far less variety than the banquets of dukes or merchants. Typical peasant fare in many regions included:

- **Rye or barley bread** (wheat bread was for the wealthy).
- A **pottage** of vegetables like onions, cabbage, turnips, or beans.
- Occasionally salted pork or herrings.
- Beer, ale, or watered-down wine (depending on the region).

Seasonal shortages could lead to hunger if crops failed. While the Renaissance brought some improvement in farming tools and methods, it did not completely erase the threat of famine. Plus, peasants often had to pay heavy taxes or rents. Hence, the difference between the diet of a noble in Florence or a merchant in Antwerp and that of a rural farmer remained enormous.

Regional Differences in Renaissance Europe

While Italy is often spotlighted, other parts of Europe also had unique Renaissance food developments:

1. **Germany and the Holy Roman Empire**: Beer brewing improved in cities, with certain regions famous for specific styles. Rich nobles ate roast game meats, dumplings, and spiced sauces, while peasants stuck to rye bread and soups.

2. **Iberian Peninsula (Spain and Portugal)**: The Reconquista ended in 1492, uniting much of Spain under Christian monarchs. Spices, sugar, and rice from earlier Arabic influences remained popular. Paella-like rice dishes developed in some areas. Portugal's maritime explorations led to new contacts with Africa, India, and beyond.

3. **England**: The Tudor period (Henry VIII, Elizabeth I) saw the aristocracy enjoying large roasts of beef, mutton, or venison. Spiced fruit pies and puddings appeared. But barley bread and pottages dominated for the poor.

4. **Low Countries (Belgium, Netherlands)**: Prosperous cities like Antwerp or Bruges traded widely. Waffles and sweet pastries gained fame. Herring and cheese became important exports, fueling both local diets and commerce.

In every case, **social class** shaped diets. Nobles, merchants, and church leaders had the means to experiment with new ingredients. Artisans and peasants made do with simpler, locally sourced fare.

Artistic Depictions of Food

One interesting aspect of the Renaissance was the **growth of painting** and the new focus on **realistic detail**. Artists like **Giuseppe Arcimboldo** created whimsical portraits using arrangements of fruits and vegetables. Others painted tavern scenes or still-life images of game, fish, and table settings. These artworks provide modern historians with glimpses of what people ate, how they presented it, and how they viewed food culturally.

Some still-life paintings showed bright lemons, oranges, or exotic peppers—revealing that these items were known and admired, at least among artists and patrons who could afford them. The presence of these foods in paintings does not mean they were common on everyone's table, but it underlines the fascination wealthy patrons had with new or imported foods.

Cookbooks and Culinary Writing

The Renaissance saw the creation of some **early printed cookbooks**, thanks to the invention of the printing press in the mid-15th century. In Italy, for instance, **Bartolomeo Scappi** (personal chef to several popes) wrote a famous cookbook in the 16th century describing hundreds of recipes, from roasts to pastries. He detailed kitchen equipment, recommended methods for preserving and flavoring foods, and discussed feast planning for large gatherings.

These cookbooks often targeted **professional cooks** or wealthy households. They listed recipes requiring sugar, spices, or complex sauces—ingredients beyond the reach of the common person. Still, such texts helped spread ideas from one city or court to another. Over time, certain "renaissance" dishes or styles found their way into royal courts across Europe, shaping the beginnings of an international aristocratic cuisine.

The Dawn of Food Exploration

By the late Renaissance, European ships sailed far into the **Atlantic** and around **Africa**. Soon, news of **new lands** across the ocean reached Europe. Although our focus is not on modern times, it is worth noting that by the end of the Renaissance, a huge exchange of crops between the Old World and the New World had begun—maize, tomatoes, potatoes, cacao, and more. Initially, these products arrived in small quantities and were viewed with curiosity or suspicion. But we will not fully explore this "Columbian Exchange" here, since it carries us closer to modern history. For the Renaissance period itself, the main developments in food came from within Europe or from older trade links with Asia and the Middle East.

Renaissance Food Legacy

Though the Renaissance did not drastically change the diets of everyday farmers, it did bring significant shifts to Europe's **upper-class cooking**. Courtly cuisine became more elegant, more experimental with spices and sugar, and more influenced by ideas of balance (from ancient texts). The growth of trade, especially in the Mediterranean, brought in new ingredients. Cookbooks began to circulate, and the arts celebrated rich displays of food.

These changes laid the **foundation** for later developments in Early Modern Europe, when colonial expansion would introduce American crops on a larger scale, and the concept of refined dining would spread further. The Renaissance was a time of **transition**: from medieval traditions to a more global awareness of ingredients and a more artistic presentation of meals. In the next chapter, we will see how the **Spice Routes** themselves shaped not only the Renaissance but also the centuries that followed, connecting multiple continents with vibrant culinary exchanges.

CHAPTER 18

The Spice Routes and Their Influence

In earlier chapters, we frequently mentioned **spices**—such as pepper, cloves, cinnamon, and nutmeg—and how they traveled to Europe along long trade routes. The demand for these items was so great that they shaped entire economies, inspired voyages of exploration, and contributed to the fortunes of cities and merchants. The term **"Spice Routes"** (or "Spice Roads") refers to the sea and land paths that linked Asia, the Middle East, East Africa, and Europe, carrying valuable spices, aromatics, and other luxury goods.

This chapter focuses on these routes, why spices were so prized, how they were traded, and what effects they had on food and culture in the regions they touched. We will see that spices were far more than flavor enhancers: they represented wealth, power, and even mystique, forging links across continents.

Why Were Spices So Valuable?

In ancient and medieval times, **spices** had multiple uses:

1. **Flavor**: Adding taste to otherwise bland or repetitive diets.
2. **Preservation**: Some believed strong spices helped preserve or disguise slightly spoiled meats, though salt and drying were more critical for actual preservation.
3. **Medicine**: Many spices were thought to have healing properties or balance the body's humors.
4. **Perfume and Ritual**: Incense, fragrant oils, or spiced drinks were used in religious or royal ceremonies.
5. **Symbol of Status**: Displaying spices in banquets or owning them signaled wealth and sophistication.

Because spices grew in specific tropical climates—like the **Maluku Islands (Spice Islands) in present-day Indonesia**, India's Malabar Coast, or areas of Sri Lanka—transporting them to distant markets required long, risky journeys. Each step in the chain added costs, making spices extremely expensive by the time they reached buyers in places like Venice or Paris.

Early Spice Routes: Overland and Maritime

For centuries, caravans carried spices overland via the **Silk Road** across Central Asia to the Middle East, then on to Mediterranean ports. Sea routes also developed: Indian Ocean traders sailed from the Malabar Coast to the Persian Gulf or Red Sea. Cities such as **Alexandria** in Egypt or **Constantinople** in Byzantium became major gateways to Europe.

During the Middle Ages, Italian city-states—**Venice**, **Genoa**, and others—controlled much of the spice trade in the Mediterranean. They imported pepper, cloves, nutmeg, and other goods, then sold them to distributors across Europe. Because these spices were so dear, the profits could be huge, fueling the wealth of powerful merchant families.

Arab and **Persian** traders were also key players, carrying spices from Southeast Asia to Middle Eastern markets. Along the way, they spread cultural influences, introducing new recipes or cooking methods to places like the Levant, Persia, and East Africa.

Spice Production Regions

Different spices come from different plants, each native to certain areas:

- **Black Pepper**: Grown on vines in tropical forests of India's Malabar Coast.

- **Cloves**: Harvested from flower buds of an evergreen tree native to the Maluku Islands in Indonesia.

- **Nutmeg and Mace**: Both from the nutmeg tree's seed and covering, also mainly found in the Maluku region.

- **Cinnamon**: Sourced from the inner bark of certain tree species in Sri Lanka (Ceylon) and parts of India.

- **Ginger**: A rhizome cultivated in India, Southeast Asia, and parts of China.

- **Cardamom**: Grown in India's Western Ghats and other tropical areas.

Because these plants thrived in remote tropical climates, European or Middle Eastern traders had to rely on local producers. In many coastal ports, kings or local rulers taxed the spice harvest, maintaining strict control over who could buy or sell. This monopoly or near-monopoly contributed to the high prices.

Spice Demand in Medieval and Renaissance Europe

In medieval and Renaissance times, the desire for spices was so great that cooks in noble households often included them in **meat dishes, sauces, pies, and pastries**. Pepper was the most widespread, but **ginger, cinnamon, cloves, nutmeg, and saffron** (from crocus flowers) were also common in wealthy kitchens. Spices gave a sweet-sour or sweet-spicy twist to meats, fish, or fruit dishes.

For everyday people, spices remained rare. They might use small amounts of pepper or local herbs. But for the wealthy, spices became a status symbol. A noble could impress guests by serving heavily spiced roasts, sweet wine with cloves and cinnamon (hypocras), or pastries colored yellow with saffron. Owning a chest of precious spices was akin to owning gold or jewels.

The Role of the Portuguese and Spanish Voyages

By the late 15th century, European powers—especially **Portugal**—wanted a direct sea route to Asia's spice sources. The high prices of land-carried spices, plus conflicts in the eastern Mediterranean, encouraged explorers to seek alternatives. **Prince Henry the Navigator** supported expeditions down the African coast. Eventually, **Vasco da Gama** reached India in 1498, opening a new maritime spice route.

Soon, the **Portuguese** established forts along the Indian Ocean, attempting to control spice ports. They seized parts of the Malabar Coast and pushed into the **Spice Islands**. The Spanish, meanwhile, sailed west, hoping to reach Asia that way, leading to the voyages of **Christopher Columbus**. While Columbus never found the Spice Islands, he encountered the Americas instead—a pivotal event in world history.

However, in this chapter, we focus on how the Spice Routes connected continents rather than the later colonization. Over time, competition among Europeans (Portuguese, Spanish, Dutch, English) intensified as each sought dominance in the spice trade. This scramble affected local producers, who had to navigate deals and conflicts with the newcomers.

Influence on Food Beyond Europe

Spice routes weren't just about Europe. **Spices** traveled to the Middle East, North Africa, East Africa, and Asia itself. In these lands, spices had been used for centuries or even millennia. However, the rising demand and higher prices in Europe sometimes increased local production or changed the balance of trade.

Arab and Persian merchants, who had long controlled sections of the Indian Ocean spice trade, found themselves competing with Portuguese armed fleets. Over time, new shipping lanes changed local economies. Meanwhile, East African ports like **Sofala** or **Mombasa** traded gold, ivory, and local produce in exchange for Asian textiles and spices, forging a rich blend of **Swahili** culture that combined African, Arab, and Persian elements.

In places like **India** itself, the presence of European trading posts introduced new relationships. Some Indian rulers welcomed the chance to tax or profit from trade, while others resented interference. Spices like pepper or cardamom remained crucial to Indian cuisine, but now they also fueled global trade patterns.

Changes in Cuisine and Culture Through Spice Trade

1. **Culinary Fusions**: As spices arrived in new lands, cooks experimented with local ingredients. For instance, Persian stews might incorporate Indian spices; North African tagines gained saffron or ginger; European pies mixed sugar with cinnamon or cloves.

2. **Rise of Confectionery**: With sugar from Mediterranean plantations or Asia, and spices from the East, sweet spiced treats became popular among the wealthy—like **gingerbread**, **marzipan**, or **spice cakes**.

3. **Medicinal Ideas**: European apothecaries sold spices as cures for various ailments. A pinch of cinnamon, a spoon of ginger, or a dose of pepper might be prescribed for colds, stomach troubles, or fatigue.

4. **Social Practices**: Tea (in Asia), coffee (in the Middle East and later Europe), or spiced wines changed how people socialized. Although tea and coffee gained more ground after our Renaissance focus, the early spice routes laid the groundwork for these beverages' spread.

Managing Supply and Demand

While the spice trade was lucrative, it was also **dangerous**. Voyages could be lost to storms, piracy, or local conflicts. Overland caravans faced desert heat, bandits, or heavy tolls. This rarity and risk explained high prices. Nations or merchant guilds that controlled a chunk of the spice flow became very rich.

In some cases, local producers were forced into **monopolies** by foreign powers. For example, the **Dutch** later tried to monopolize clove production in the Maluku Islands by destroying trees on islands they didn't control. But that is partly post-Renaissance. Even during the Renaissance, competition among Venice, Genoa, Portuguese explorers, and Ottoman traders showed how critical control over spice routes could be. Spices were not just flavor—they were politics.

Spices in Ritual and Celebration

Across cultures, spices often featured in **religious or festive events**. For example:

- **Incense** (frankincense and myrrh) burned in Christian, Jewish, or other religious ceremonies, symbolizing prayers rising to the heavens.

- In Hindu traditions, various spices and fragrant substances played roles in offerings or pujas.

- In the Islamic world, spiced sweets or scented waters appeared during celebrations like Eid.

Additionally, spices used in wedding feasts or royal coronations demonstrated generosity and wealth. A spiced wine served at the end of a banquet might symbolize hospitality and good fortune.

European Expansion of Taste

Before direct sea routes, Europe's reliance on Middle Eastern intermediaries kept spice prices high. After sea routes opened, some prices dropped, making moderate amounts of pepper or cinnamon more accessible to well-off middle-class families, not just royalty. Still, spices remained a **luxury**—a little pepper on the table was a sign of respect and status. Over time, the spice craze influenced European palates, favoring sweet-and-spicy combinations in many dishes, from meat sauces to fruit pies.

Later centuries would see even more profound changes, like the arrival of **chili peppers** from the Americas, which changed cooking in India, the Middle East, and beyond. But that belongs to a slightly later era than the core Renaissance. For now, we note that the essential role of the Spice Routes was to bridge distant lands, allowing flavors from tropical Asia to transform dining from the Middle East to Europe.

Long-Term Effects of the Spice Routes

By connecting producers in tropical Asia with consumers in the Middle East, Europe, and Africa, the **Spice Routes** laid the groundwork for a more interconnected world. They impacted:

1. **Economics**: Certain ports became wealthy hubs (Venice, Malacca, Calicut, Alexandria).
2. **Politics**: Struggles over access to spice-producing regions shaped alliances, wars, and treaties.
3. **Culinary Traditions**: Cooks worldwide developed new recipes, mixing local foods with exotic seasonings.
4. **Cultural Exchange**: Traders brought stories, religious ideas, technologies, and artistic styles along with spices.

In time, these routes would become part of a larger global trade network, especially once European powers established permanent colonies and the Americas entered the mix. But as we focus on the Middle Ages and Renaissance, it is enough to say that the **Spice Routes** were a key driver of wealth, exploration, and cultural blending. They quite literally "spiced up" the diets of kings, queens, merchants, and eventually the rising middle class.

CHAPTER 19

Early Colonial Era Foods

The **Early Colonial Era** began when European powers started establishing colonies in the Americas, parts of Africa, and Asia. While there is no single date for all places, this period broadly covers the **16th to 18th centuries**, overlapping with the late Renaissance and continuing into the early modern period. During this time, major sea voyages and settlements caused huge changes in the world's food supply.

In this chapter, we will explore how **Europeans** established colonies in the **New World** (the Americas), how **African** peoples were forcibly brought to the Americas through the **Atlantic slave trade**, and how **Asian** trade posts impacted farming and cooking. We will see a **global exchange** of crops—like potatoes, maize, sugarcane—and the introduction of livestock to new lands. While many of these changes were shaped by conflict, forced labor, and the expansion of empires, the effect on food history was enormous.

The Columbian Exchange: A Worldwide Swap of Foods

When we talk about colonial foods, we have to mention the **Columbian Exchange**. This term describes the movement of **plants, animals, and diseases** between the Old World (Europe, Asia, Africa) and the New World (the Americas) after 1492. Although we touched on the beginnings of this exchange in earlier chapters, the **Early Colonial Era** saw it grow drastically.

- **From the Americas** to the Old World came: maize (corn), tomatoes, potatoes, chili peppers, cacao (chocolate), peanuts, squash, and more.

- **From the Old World** to the Americas came: wheat, rice, sugarcane, coffee, horses, cattle, pigs, sheep, chickens, and a variety of fruits (like oranges and bananas, though bananas themselves originated in Asia and Africa).

This exchange transformed diets on both sides of the Atlantic. Potatoes and corn became staples in parts of Europe, Africa, and Asia, while wheat, cattle, and sugar plantations changed food landscapes in the Americas. People often do not realize how recent these crops and animals are to certain regions. Before Europeans arrived in the Americas, there were **no horses** or **cattle** there; likewise, Europeans did not know tomatoes or cacao.

Colonialism in the Americas: Settlements and Plantation Foods

Spain, **Portugal**, **England**, **France**, and the **Dutch** established colonies throughout the Americas. Spanish colonies covered much of Latin America, Portuguese colonies centered on Brazil, and the English, French, and Dutch took parts of North America and the Caribbean. Each region had unique interactions between the colonizers and the indigenous populations.

Spanish Colonies

- **Encomienda System**: Spanish settlers received land and labor from local native communities, though this was often abusive. Indigenous farming methods, like maize cultivation, influenced Spanish settlers.

- **Food Blends**: In Mexico and Peru, Spaniards introduced wheat and livestock (cattle, pigs, goats), while adopting local crops like maize, chili peppers, tomatoes, and potatoes. Over time, dishes mixing Spanish meats with Mesoamerican or Andean ingredients became common—leading to the foundations of many Latin American cuisines.

- **Sugar Plantations**: In the Caribbean and coastal areas, the Spanish established sugarcane plantations, which required intensive labor often forced on enslaved Africans or indigenous peoples.

Portuguese Colonies (Especially Brazil)

- **Sugar**: Brazil became a major sugarcane producer. Plantations (engenhos) relied heavily on enslaved labor brought from Africa.

- **Cattle Ranching**: Over time, cattle were introduced to vast grasslands. The local population blended European meats with native fruits and tubers, gradually creating unique Brazilian dishes.

- **Cassava (Manioc)**: An important native root crop in Brazil, which Portuguese colonists also adopted. It could be processed into **farinha** (flour) or **tapioca**.

English, French, and Dutch Colonies in North America and the Caribbean

- **Tobacco and Food Crops**: In places like Virginia, tobacco became the big cash crop, but colonists also grew **maize**, **beans**, and **squash** learned from Native Americans. Wheat and barley were introduced too.

- **Caribbean Plantations**: The English, French, and Dutch seized islands where sugarcane thrived. They built large plantations, importing enslaved Africans to do the labor. This created a blend of African, European, and indigenous cooking styles in the Caribbean—spicy stews, fried plantains, rice-based dishes, and more.

- **Fur Trade**: In northern areas (New France, parts of English territories), the economy centered on trading furs with indigenous peoples. Foods in these colder climates included the adaptation of local fish, game, berries, and eventually introduced cereals (wheat, oats).

In all these colonies, the daily food of colonists varied by class. Wealthy plantation owners might have elaborate meals with imported goods like wine, refined flour, or spices, while poorer settlers and workers survived on simpler staples—often combining Old and New World ingredients in stews, breads, and porridges.

Enslaved Africans and Their Culinary Influence

One of the most tragic aspects of the Early Colonial Era was the **Atlantic slave trade**, where millions of Africans were forcibly taken to the Americas to work on plantations. Despite the brutality, these enslaved Africans brought with them profound knowledge of farming and cooking.

- **African Crops in the Americas**: Many enslaved people knew how to grow rice (from West African traditions), leading to the development of rice plantations in places like South Carolina. Crops like okra, black-eyed peas, yams, and certain melons also made their way into American fields.

- **Cooking Methods**: African cooking styles influenced local cuisines—stewing, frying, spicing with peppers, and using leafy greens. Dishes like **gumbo** in Louisiana or **feijoada** in Brazil have roots in African, indigenous, and Portuguese traditions.

- **Cuisine as Survival and Culture**: Enslaved communities often received poor-quality rations—like leftover pork parts or fish heads—yet they created tasty, sustaining dishes by blending African spices, local produce, and cooking techniques. These foods became part of the cultural heritage in the Americas, from the Caribbean to the southern United States to Brazil.

Despite the horrors of slavery, African contributions to agriculture, livestock care, and cooking styles were central to the colonial food systems, shaping entire regional cuisines that still exist today.

Cultural Exchange with Indigenous Peoples

Wherever Europeans settled, they encountered indigenous peoples with deep knowledge of local crops and ecosystems. Some exchanges were **peaceful**, like the Pilgrims learning to grow maize from the Wampanoag in early Plymouth

Colony, or French fur traders adopting native methods of preserving foods. Other interactions were violent or exploitative, with colonizers seizing land and resources.

Still, the influence of indigenous crops on colonial diets was massive:

- **Maize (Corn)**: Became a staple for colonists in many regions of North and South America.

- **Beans, Squashes, and Pumpkins**: Provided vitamins and nutrients.

- **Maple Syrup** (Northeastern North America): Native peoples tapped maple trees for sap, an idea colonists adopted to sweeten foods.

- **Tropical Fruits**: In places like the Amazon or the Caribbean, local fruits—pineapples, guava, papaya—joined colonial tables, mixing with European pastries or sweet preserves.

However, the severe decline of indigenous populations (due to disease, war, and displacement) often meant that colonial societies only partially adopted native foodways. Nevertheless, from southern chili-based stews to northern cornbreads, the mark of indigenous agriculture remains in many modern cuisines.

Livestock and Farming Transformations

Horses, cattle, pigs, goats, and chickens did not exist in the Americas before European arrival. Once introduced, they thrived in many environments:

- **Cattle ranches** spread across the pampas of South America (Argentina, Uruguay) and the Great Plains of North America, although native bison herds were also present.

- **Horses** revolutionized the lives of some indigenous groups, like the Plains tribes (Lakota, Cheyenne, Comanche), who became master horsemen for hunting bison.

- **Pigs** multiplied rapidly in warm climates, sometimes going feral and impacting local ecosystems.

In Africa, the exchange also occurred: crops like maize and cassava from the Americas became staples in many regions, boosting populations but sometimes changing local farming methods. Meanwhile, Asia's role included adding new vegetables or adopting American peppers and corn in places like China and India (though that process continued more into the 17th and 18th centuries).

Colonial Cities and Marketplaces

By the 17th and 18th centuries, major colonial **cities** appeared:

- **Mexico City** (on the site of Tenochtitlan), with sprawling markets featuring both Spanish-introduced wheat and native chili peppers.

- **Lima** in Peru, capital of the Viceroyalty, linking Andean potato fields with Spanish wheat and African influences.
- **Havana** in Cuba, a hub for sugar, tobacco, and enslaved labor.

- **Boston** and **Philadelphia** in the English colonies, with a mix of English grains, local game, and some African-influenced dishes.

- **Rio de Janeiro** in Brazil, shipping sugar, gold, coffee (introduced later), and receiving enslaved Africans.

Markets sold a blend of Old and New World foods: wheat flour, maize, cassava, beef, pork, tropical fruits, beans, rice, and sugar. Merchants, indigenous farmers, enslaved cooks, and European settlers all interacted, creating complex new culinary traditions in these urban melting pots.

Sugar, Coffee, and Cocoa: Plantation Crops

Three crops became especially important in colonial plantations:

1. **Sugarcane**: Grown primarily in the Caribbean and Brazil. Processing sugar involved cutting cane, crushing it in mills, and boiling the juice to form crystals. This labor-intensive process relied heavily on enslaved workers. Sugar was a luxury in Europe but became increasingly demanded for sweet pastries, confections, and later, tea or coffee.

2. **Coffee**: Native to Africa (Ethiopia), coffee spread to the Middle East, then to European markets. In the early colonial era, the Dutch and French established coffee plantations in their tropical colonies (e.g., in the Caribbean or Southeast Asia). Over time, coffee drinking soared in Europe.

3. **Cocoa (Cacao)**: Native to Mesoamerica, cacao was cultivated by indigenous peoples. The Spanish realized the value of chocolate, sweetened it with cane sugar, and introduced it to Europe as a luxury drink. Colonists expanded cacao plantations in places like Venezuela or Ecuador, again often using forced labor.

These plantation crops not only changed diets around the world—people drank sweetened chocolate, coffee, or tea—but also shaped entire colonial economies, leading to wealth for some and suffering for many enslaved people.

Religious Orders and Missionary Influence on Food

Various religious orders—like the Jesuits, Franciscans, Dominicans—operated in the colonies, founding **missions** to convert indigenous peoples to Christianity. These missions also introduced European farming methods. They often built **mission gardens** growing Old World herbs, vines, cereals, and orchard fruits, alongside local crops. In some parts of the Americas (like California under Spanish rule), missions became centers where grapes, olives, and wheat were cultivated.

Missionaries sometimes tried to replace local religious feasts with Christian celebrations, but over time, many indigenous or African food traditions blended with Christian holidays. For instance, certain Catholic feast days might incorporate local dishes or ingredients into the celebratory meals. This syncretism is still visible in many Latin American festivals.

Influence in Asia and Africa Beyond the Americas

While much colonial focus was on the Americas, Europeans also established **trading posts** or partial colonies in **Asia** (like the Portuguese in Goa, India, or Macau, China) and in parts of **Africa** (like coastal Angola or Mozambique for the Portuguese, or the Dutch at the Cape Colony). These footholds introduced:

- **American crops** like maize, peanuts, and chili peppers to Africa and parts of Asia. Africa's population grew partly thanks to the caloric benefits of maize and cassava.

- **European livestock** to certain coastal areas.

- **Mixed cuisines**: In places like Goa, local Indian cooking blended with Portuguese ingredients (vinegar, pork, wine-based sauces), creating unique dishes like vindaloo.

Though not always recognized in older histories, Africans and Asians also influenced these interactions, shaping how the new crops were grown or integrated into local diets. The forced movement of enslaved Africans to Asia was smaller but still occurred in some regions, further adding to cultural exchange.

Daily Life and Food for Settlers and Workers

Most ordinary colonists—farmers, artisans, laborers—ate simpler diets than the wealthy plantation or mine owners. They often combined Old World staples (wheat bread, salted cod, pork) with local produce (maize, beans, cassava, tropical fruits). Over time, staple dishes emerged:

- **Arepas** (corn cakes) in parts of Spanish America.

- **Feijoada** (bean and meat stew) in Portuguese Brazil, originally from enslaved communities.
- **Gumbo** or **jambalaya** in French Louisiana, blending African, French, and native influences.
- **Pemmican** or **cornmeal-based** stews in English or French North America, adapted from indigenous preservation or cooking methods.

Class and status meant the difference between elaborate feasts featuring imported wines, refined sugar confections, and roast meats, versus meager meals of corn mush or cassava bread for indentured servants or enslaved people. Disease and malnutrition were common in harsh colonial settings, especially on plantations or in mining regions.

The Lasting Impact of Early Colonial Foods

By the end of the 18th century, the **global food map** had changed drastically. Crops like **maize, potatoes, chili peppers, tomatoes, and cassava**—once strictly American—were grown widely across Europe, Africa, and Asia. Livestock like **cattle, horses, pigs, and sheep** were common in the Americas. **Sugar, coffee, and cacao** fueled plantation economies, linking continents through commerce and exploitation.

The Early Colonial Era laid the basis for modern global cuisines. For example:

- Italy's tomato-based sauces or northern Europe's widespread potato dishes would not exist without American crops.
- West African stews with peanuts or chili peppers reflect the introduction of New World plants.
- Caribbean cooking (jerk seasonings, plantains, callaloo) is a blend of African, Taino, Spanish, and other influences.

All these transformations stemmed from the massive movements of people, animals, and plants during colonization—often driven by the quest for profit and empire-building. While it enriched some, it brought terrible suffering to others, especially indigenous and enslaved African populations. Yet from a **purely culinary** standpoint, the mixing of foods from different continents created entirely new flavors and dishes, shaping the meals billions enjoy today.

CHAPTER 20

Food at the Dawn of the Industrial Age

By the **late 18th and early 19th centuries**, many of the processes we have discussed—from ancient farming to the colonial exchange of crops—were well established. People around the world ate combinations of local and introduced foods. But a new era was about to begin: the **Industrial Age**, which would bring machines, steam power, and mass production techniques to fields and kitchens. In this final chapter, we will examine what food looked like at the **Dawn of the Industrial Age**, just before major inventions reshaped agriculture and cooking.

Historical Context: Late 18th to Early 19th Centuries

In regions like **Europe** and parts of **North America**, economies were shifting from feudal or colonial systems toward early capitalism. Political revolutions—like the **American Revolution** (1775–1783) and the **French Revolution** (1789–1799)—changed social structures, while Enlightenment ideas questioned old hierarchies. Some societies began inventing **steam engines**, **spinning machines**, and other mechanical devices. This period precedes the full-blown Industrial Revolution, which took off in the mid-19th century.

Meanwhile, overseas colonies still thrived: sugar plantations in the Caribbean, cotton in the American South, coffee in Latin America, and so on. The **Atlantic slave trade** continued, though challenges to slavery began growing in some parts of Europe and North America. Agricultural improvements, such as the **Enclosure Movement** in England and better crop rotation, increased food production, but also displaced many small farmers.

Key question for us: How did all these changes affect what people ate?

Agriculture on the Eve of Mechanization

Most farming worldwide still relied on **human labor** and **animal power**—oxen or horses pulling plows, people planting and harvesting by hand. There were no tractors yet, though some **seed drills** and mechanical harvesters (like those designed by Jethro Tull or Cyrus McCormick slightly later) were in experimental stages.

New Crop Rotations: Farmers in parts of Europe replaced the medieval three-field system with more advanced rotations, including legumes (clover, peas) that replenished the soil. This boosted yields and allowed larger herds of livestock, as clover made good animal feed. More animals meant more **manure**, further improving soil fertility.

Selective Breeding: Innovators like **Robert Bakewell** in England applied ideas of controlled breeding to produce bigger sheep or cattle. This meant more meat and better wool or milk. While these methods were still early, they pointed to a shift from small-scale subsistence to more commercially oriented farming.

Still, the majority of people in rural areas grew enough for their family or local market. Hunger and famine could happen if harvests failed—witness the **Irish Potato Famine** (1840s), which came slightly after our period but was rooted in the reliance on a single crop. People everywhere looked for ways to secure stable food supplies, but the technology was not yet advanced to guarantee it.

Urbanization and Food Markets

As factories and mills emerged, **urban centers** began to grow. More people left the countryside to seek work in towns. This created demand for **market gardens** near cities, which supplied fresh produce—vegetables, dairy, eggs—while grains and meats came from farther away.

In places like **London, Paris, or New York**, large markets sold bread, meat, fish, and seasonal fruits. Street vendors offered quick meals of pies, hot eels, roasted chestnuts, or boiled corn, depending on local tastes. However, **refrigeration** did not exist in modern form, so fresh foods had to be consumed quickly. Salting, smoking, drying, or pickling remained essential for preservation.

Wealthy city dwellers might still enjoy elaborate multi-course meals, but the rising **middle class** sought simpler, hearty fare. Cookbooks and household guides taught housewives how to manage a respectable table on a moderate budget, focusing on roasts, stews, puddings, and breads. Many people lived in crowded conditions, so they relied on local bakers, butchers, and grocers for daily supplies.

The Continuing Influence of Colonial Products

By the dawn of the Industrial Age, **colonial goods** like sugar, tea, coffee, and chocolate had become more common in Europe and North America (though still somewhat costly). Sugar, once a rare luxury, now sweetened teas and pastries more regularly for the middle class. Coffee houses had already been popular gathering spots in cities like London or Paris since the 17th century. Tea was a mainstay in Britain and some of its colonies.

Chocolate drinks evolved into confections, though chocolate bars would only appear much later. Tobacco (from the Americas) also spread widely, influencing social habits. Over time, enslaved labor on plantations still produced much of the sugar and coffee supply, though movements to abolish slavery were gaining traction in Britain and elsewhere (Britain outlawed the slave trade in 1807, slavery in 1833).

Spices like pepper, cloves, nutmeg, and cinnamon were more accessible than before, although still not cheap. They no longer dominated elite cuisine as in the Middle Ages, since tastes shifted to more delicate herb-based seasonings. However, pepper remained widespread, and sweet spices were popular in baked goods or holiday puddings.

Diet of the Working Classes

The early Industrial Age saw the rise of factory work, especially in textile mills. Workers often toiled for long hours, earning low wages. Their diets could be **monotonous**:

- **Bread or porridge** from cheap grains.

- **Potatoes** in regions where they had become a staple (Ireland, parts of Scotland, Germany).

- **Tea** or **small beer** for hydration, as fresh water was sometimes polluted in urban areas.

- **Occasional meat** (often salted or fatty cuts) if wages allowed.

- **Few vegetables** besides onions or cabbage, though some might grow small kitchen gardens if space was available.

Poor living conditions in rapidly growing industrial cities led to concerns about malnutrition and disease. Meanwhile, wealthy industrialists and the upper classes enjoyed more varied diets, often influenced by new cookbook trends or by hiring specialized cooks who prepared multi-course meals. This sharp divide in food quality and access foreshadowed the social and labor movements of the 19th century.

Changing Cooking Technology (Before Modern Machines)

While we did not yet have electric stoves or gas ovens, small innovations did appear:

- **Cast Iron Stoves**: Replacing open hearths in some middle-class and upper-class homes. This allowed more controlled baking and simmering, though open fires remained standard in poorer households or rural areas for a long time.

- **Metal Cookware**: Copper or cast iron pots were prized, though they required care. Cheaper iron pots became more available with improved metalworking.

- **Kitchen Gadgets**: Simple mechanical devices like coffee grinders, pepper mills, or pastry crimpers. Hand-cranked churns for butter might appear on some farms.

Baking in professional or communal ovens was still common, especially in Europe, where families might bring dough to a local baker. In North America, wood-burning stoves eventually spread, making home baking easier. But all these changes were gradual, with wide variations from place to place.

Culinary Ideas and Cookbooks

By the **late 18th century**, more cookbooks were being published, often directed at **middle-class housewives**. For instance, in England, Hannah Glasse wrote *The Art of Cookery Made Plain and Easy* (first published 1747), instructing readers on roasts, pies, and puddings with simpler language than earlier aristocratic texts. In France, cookbooks described the refined cooking of noble or bourgeois families, using butter, cream, wine sauces, and fresh herbs rather than heavy medieval spices.

Enlightenment thinkers sometimes wrote about nutrition, linking it to health or moral character. However, scientific understanding of vitamins or calories did not yet exist. People recognized that a varied diet was healthier than one of stale bread and watery soup, but they could not explain it with modern science. Physicians still leaned on **humoral theories** or basic observation, recommending "light" or "heavy" foods for certain ailments.

Regional Snapshots

1. **England**: The diet of a wealthy English household might include daily bread from wheat flour, morning tea or coffee, midday roast beef or mutton with root vegetables, and puddings or pies. The working classes ate more coarse bread, onions, cheese, and beer. Potatoes gained ground, but not all regions accepted them quickly (some suspicious of the "strange root").
2. **France**: Upper-class cuisine evolved into lighter sauces (gravies) and the concept of "courses." Bourgeois families might have stewed meats with wine, vegetable ragouts, and pastries. Rural peasants lived on dark bread, soup, and occasional pork or chicken.
3. **Germany/Prussia**: Rye bread, sausages, cabbage, and beer were staples. Potatoes introduced by Frederick the Great in the mid-18th century gradually became a mainstay.
4. **North America**: In the newly formed United States, diets varied by region—New Englanders consumed baked beans, brown bread, fish chowders; the South relied more on cornmeal (hoecakes), pork, and eventually black-eyed peas or okra from African influences. Frontier settlers hunted game and grew maize.
5. **Latin America**: Under Spanish or Portuguese rule, big estates produced wheat (in cooler highlands), sugar, coffee, or cocoa. Indigenous peoples in rural areas still favored maize tortillas, Andean potatoes, or cassava, but might adopt European livestock or wheat bread.
6. **Asia**: Though large parts of Asia were not colonized in the same way (except for certain enclaves), trade connections meant that American crops like chili peppers, corn, and peanuts were integrated into local

cuisines (e.g., Sichuan chili dishes in China, the use of peanuts in Southeast Asia). Rice remained dominant, but commercial crops like tea expanded for export.

Social Classes and Food Access

The **difference** between the wealthy, middle class, and poor was stark. Aristocrats still hosted elaborate banquets with silver servingware and multiple courses. The rising **middle class** sought to imitate some of this style on a smaller scale, perhaps serving a roast on Sundays. The poor, including many factory workers, farm laborers, and the rural underclass, ate heavily on bread, potatoes, or porridge, with minimal meat or fresh vegetables. Malnutrition was common among child workers, leading to stunted growth or illness.

Some philanthropic groups and early social reformers recognized that factory workers lacked enough healthy food. They wrote reports describing poor diets, but major reforms would come only in the mid- to late 19th century. Similarly, the movement to abolish slavery gained momentum, but enslaved labor still produced large amounts of sugar and cotton in the early 1800s, shaping diets overseas.

Banquets and Entertaining

Among the upper classes, the **banquet** or **dinner party** remained a social highlight. More specialized roles appeared in noble or wealthy households: a **chef** (or "head cook"), a pastry cook, scullery maids, etc. The meal might be served **à la française**, with many dishes on the table at once, or transitioning toward **à la russe**, where dishes arrive in courses (this shift grew in popularity in the 19th century).

Servants wore liveries or uniforms, carrying polished platters of roast duck, beef, or fish. Vegetables included peas, beans, carrots, or cauliflower, sometimes new horticultural varieties. Desserts might be fruit tarts, sweet puddings, or shaped jellies. Wines from France, Spain, or Portugal accompanied the feast, and perhaps brandy or cordials afterward. Socializing and conversation were as important as the meal's flavors.

Culinary Currents in the Late Colonial Sphere

Though some colonies became independent states (like the USA in 1776), many were still under European powers. Foods in these regions reflected that:

- **Caribbean**: Sugar, rum (from molasses), tropical fruits, African-inspired stews. Some free communities grew their own small plots (provision grounds) with yams, plantains, or maize.

- **Spanish America**: Traditional local foods blended with Spanish influences. Chilies, beans, rice, and tortillas or arepas were common among the masses, while the upper class might enjoy Spanish-style wheat breads, wines, or pastries.

- **Brazil**: Portuguese colonial society had feijoada, cassava dishes, sugar, coffee, and a mixture of African, indigenous, and Portuguese cooking methods.

- **French Colonial**: In places like Saint-Domingue (Haiti), sugar plantations dominated. Also, coffee production took off. A blend of French sauces with African or native ingredients influenced local dishes.

By the early 19th century, some colonies were on the brink of **independence movements**. This would eventually reshape trade patterns, but for now, the old structure of plantation crops exported to Europe remained central.

Inventors and Early Machines in Food Production

Though large-scale mechanization was still limited, a few **inventors** were tinkering with devices that would change farming and food processing:

- **Canning**: The Frenchman Nicolas Appert invented a method of heating and sealing food in containers around 1809. This was initially for Napoleon's army. Early canning helped preserve foods for longer journeys, but it remained somewhat expensive and used glass or tin.

- **Seed Drills** and **Reaping Machines**: Jethro Tull's seed drill in the early 1700s and the mechanical reapers developed in the early 1800s (e.g., Cyrus McCormick's reaper) laid the groundwork for more efficient grain production.

- **Steam Mills**: Some mills for flour or sugarcane began using steam power, increasing output.

These innovations marked the dawn of industrial methods in food production. However, they were not yet universal. Most people still harvested with scythes and ground grain in local windmills or watermills. Full industrial farming would emerge later in the 19th century.

Food and Cultural Identity

At the cusp of the Industrial Age, people's sense of **national or regional identity** began to grow. Cuisine played a role in forming these identities:

- **French Cuisine**: Regarded as sophisticated, with carefully prepared sauces, pastries, and the beginnings of haute cuisine traditions.
- **English Cuisine**: Emphasized roasts, puddings, pies, and strong ales or tea.

- **Italian Cuisine**: Varied by region, featuring pasta, polenta, or risotto in the north, tomato-based sauces (still quite new) in the south. Olives, cheeses, and wine were staples, though tomatoes were not fully embraced in all areas yet.
- **Chinese Cuisine**: In a different context, had long-established cooking methods (stir-frying, steaming) using rice, noodles, vegetables, and sauces like soy sauce. Chili peppers introduced from the Americas had begun to reshape southwestern Chinese dishes.

For the most part, these identities were recognized in local or travel accounts, not in mass media. Cookbooks, travelers' diaries, or letters described "exotic" dishes or local specialties. Some aristocrats or wealthier travelers sought novelty in foreign foods, setting the stage for the global curiosity about diverse cuisines in later centuries.

The Stage Is Set for Major Changes

As we close this final chapter, we see a world where:

- People have begun using **colonial ingredients** widely. Potatoes, tomatoes, chili peppers, cacao, and more are integrated into many cuisines.

- **Sugar, coffee, and tea** have become everyday luxuries for middle classes in Europe, financed largely by colonial plantations.

- **Urbanization** and early industries create new demands for consistent food supplies, spurring better transport and farm output.

- **Social disparities** remain huge: peasants and workers often have limited diets, while aristocrats or industrial tycoons eat multi-course feasts.

- Inventors are on the verge of harnessing **steam power** and mechanical devices for food production, but the big transformations—railroads, widespread canning, refrigeration—lie just ahead in the mid- to late 19th century.

Thus, at the **Dawn of the Industrial Age**, the world's food systems are at a tipping point. The centuries of exploration, colonial exchange, and small-scale farming methods are about to give way to new technologies that will shape modern agriculture and cooking. While our story ends here—before large factories, tractors, and global shipping networks—the foundation is in place. Humanity has woven together crops and culinary ideas from every corner of the globe, setting the stage for the modern era.

Conclusion of Chapter 20 and Final Note

In **Chapter 19**, we explored how **Early Colonial Era Foods** emerged from the forced mingling of European, African, and indigenous American traditions, powered by plantation economies and the Columbian Exchange. In **Chapter 20**, we see how, on the eve of the Industrial Age, these global foods and cooking styles were firmly established but still produced and cooked by largely traditional methods. Small technological innovations hinted at a future of machine-driven farming and processing, yet for most people, daily food remained rooted in local fields and hand labor.

This concludes our **Complete History of Food** before modern industrial transformations. We have traveled from **prehistoric hunting and gathering** through the rise of ancient civilizations, medieval and Renaissance feasts, the Mongol and Silk Road exchanges, the Pre-Columbian societies, and finally to the broad changes of the Early Colonial Era and the dawn of modern mechanization. Each step showed how human creativity, cooperation, and sometimes conflict shaped what we eat. Although we stop here—on the threshold of modernity—the story of food continues, ready to enter an era of steam engines, global shipping, and beyond.

Help Us Share Your Thoughts!

Dear reader,

Thank you for spending your time with this book. We hope it brought you enjoyment and a few new ideas to think about. If there was anything that didn't work for you, or if you have suggestions on how we can improve, please let us know at **kontakt@skriuwer.com**. Your feedback means a lot to us and helps us make our books even better.

If you enjoyed this book, we would be very grateful if you left a review on the site where you purchased it. Your review not only helps other readers find our books, but also encourages us to keep creating more stories and materials that you'll love.

By choosing Skriuwer, you're also supporting **Frisian**—a minority language mainly spoken in the northern Netherlands. Although **Frisian** has a rich history, the number of speakers is shrinking, and it's at risk of dying out. Your purchase helps fund resources to preserve and promote this language, such as educational programs and learning tools. If you'd like to learn more about Frisian or even start learning it yourself, please visit **www.learnfrisian.com**.

Thank you for being part of our community. We look forward to sharing more books with you in the future.

Warm regards,
The Skriuwer Team

www.ingramcontent.com/pod-product-compliance
Lightning Source LLC
LaVergne TN
LVHW020332200726
843507LV00012B/2329